Contents

Air fryer Chicken Wings

Prep Time:	5 minutes	Calories:	168
Cook Time:	16 minutes	Fat (g):	13
Total Time:	21 minutes	Protein (g):	11
Servings:	4	Carbs (g):	0

Ingredients:

- Chicken wings
- Olive oil
- Garlic salt
- Lemon pepper

1 lb (453 g)
1 tablespoon
2 teaspoons
1 teaspoon

Instructions:

1. Switch on the air fryer, insert the fryer basket, grease it with olive oil, then set the cooking temperature to 400 degrees F (204 °C), and set frying time for 5 minutes or more to preheat the fryer.
2. Meanwhile, take a large bowl, then pat dry wings with paper towels and place them into the bowl.
3. Add all the remaining ingredients into the bowl and stir until wings evenly coated.
4. Place chicken wings into the fryer basket in a single layer, then set the cooking temperature to 400 degrees F (204 °C), adjust frying time for 16 minutes (8 minutes per side), and cook until crispy and golden brown, flipping halfway through and spraying with oil.
5. When done, transfer chicken wings onto a plate and serve.

Air fryer French Fries

Prep Time:	5 minutes	Calories:	279
Cook Time:	30 minutes	Fat (g):	0.3
Total Time:	35 minutes	Protein (g):	8
Servings:	2	Carbs (g):	62

Ingredients:

- Russet potatoes   2
- Olive oil   2 tablespoons
- Salt   2 teaspoons

Instructions:

1. Switch on the air fryer, insert the fryer basket, grease it with olive oil, then set the cooking temperature to 400 degrees F (204 °C), and set frying time for 5 minutes or more to preheat the fryer.
2. Meanwhile, slice potatoes into ¼ inch sticks.
3. Drizzle potato sticks with olive oil, sprinkle with salt and then toss to coat.
4. Place potato sticks into the fryer basket in a single layer, then set the cooking temperature to 380 degrees F (193 °C), adjust frying time for 15 minutes, and cook until crispy, flipping halfway through and spraying with oil. Cook fries in batches if needed.
5. Serve with desired dips and seasonings.

Air fryer Chicken Nuggets

Prep Time:	10 minutes	Calories:	228
Cook Time:	12 minutes	Fat (g):	5
Total Time:	22 minutes	Protein (g):	29
Servings:	4	Carbs (g):	19

Ingredients:

- Chicken breast, skinless   1
- Butter, melted   ½ cup
- Salt   1/4 teaspoon
- Black pepper   1/8 teaspoon
- Breadcrumbs   ½ cup

- Parmesan cheese, grated   2 tablespoons
- Paprika   ¼ teaspoon
- Garlic powder   ¼ teaspoon

Instructions:

1. Switch on the air fryer, insert the fryer basket, grease it with oil, then set the cooking temperature to 400 degrees F (204 °C) and set frying time for 5 minutes or more to preheat the fryer until the food is ready to cook.
2. Meanwhile, cut the chicken into nuggets shape or bite-size pieces and place them into a large bowl.
3. Season chicken pieces with salt, pepper, paprika, and garlic powder and set aside until required.
4. Place melted butter into a small bowl.
5. Place breadcrumbs and parmesan cheese into another bowl.
6. Prepare nuggets and for this, dip each chicken piece into melted butter and finally coat with breadcrumbs mixture.
7. Place chicken nuggets into the fryer basket in a single layer, then set the cooking temperature to 400 degrees F (204 °C), adjust frying time for 12 minutes, and cook until crispy, flipping halfway through and spraying with oil. Cook nuggets in batches if needed.
8. Serve with desired dips and seasonings.

Air fryer Mozzarella Sticks

Prep Time:	1 h 30 m	Calories:	48
Cook Time:	20 minutes	Fat (g):	2
Total Time:	1 h 50 m	Protein (g):	3
Servings:	24	Carbs (g):	2

Ingredients:

- Mozzarella sticks, halved — 10 oz (12 sticks)
- Whole - wheat flour — ¼ cup
- Breadcrumbs — ¼ cup
- Panko — ¼ cup
- Egg — 1

- Onion powder   1 teaspoon
- Garlic powder   1 teaspoon
- Salt   ½ teaspoon
- Chili powder   ½ teaspoon
- Paprika   ½ teaspoon

Instructions:

1. Place mozzarella sticks in a freezer for 20 minutes.
2. Meanwhile, take a small bowl, crack the egg in it, whisk well, and set aside.
3. Take a second bowl and place flour into it.
4. Take a third bowl, place all the remaining ingredients into it except for mozzarella, and mix well.
5. Take a baking sheet, line it with parchment paper. Take the frozen mozzarella sticks and then dredge them in flour, then dip sticks into the egg mixture and finally coat sticks with breadcrumbs mixture until evenly covered on all sides.
6. Place the sticks on a baking sheet and then place them in a freezer for an hour.
7. After 50 minutes, switch on the air fryer, insert the fryer basket, grease it with oil, and set the cooking temperature to 400 degrees F (204 °C). Set frying time for 5 minutes or more to preheat the fryer until the food is ready to cook.
8. Place mozzarella sticks into the fryer basket in a single layer, and set the cooking temperature to 370 degrees F (188 °C). Adjust frying time for 5 minutes and cook until crispy, flipping halfway through and spraying with oil. Cook about 6-7 mozzarella sticks at a time.
9. Serve with desired dips and seasonings.

Air fryer Onion Rings

Prep Time:	10 minutes	Calories:	193
Cook Time:	15 minutes	**Fat (g):**	8
Total Time:	25 minutes	**Protein (g):**	4
Servings:	2	**Carbs (g):**	26

Ingredients:

- All-purpose flour   ½ cup
- Buttermilk   ½ cup
- Paprika   1 teaspoon
- Salt   1 teaspoon

- Egg   1
- Panko   1 cup
- Onion, large   1
- Olive oil   2 tablespoons

Instructions:

1. Switch on the air fryer, insert the fryer basket, grease it with oil, then set the cooking temperature to 400 degrees F (204 °C) and set frying time for 5 minutes or more to preheat the fryer until the food is ready to cook.
2. Meanwhile, slice the onion about ½-inch thick, divide it into rings, and place them into a large bowl.
3. Place flour, paprika, and ½ teaspoon of salt into a first bowl and mix well.
4. In another bowl, place buttermilk, egg, and ¼ cup of the flour mixture and mix well.
5. Take a third bowl and place panko, olive oil, and remaining salt into it and mix well.
6. Prepare onion rings, and for this, dredge each ring in the flour mixture, then drop them into the buttermilk mixture, and finally coat with the panko mixture.
7. Place onion rings into the fryer basket in a single layer, then set the cooking temperature to 400 degrees F (204 °C), adjust frying time for 13-15 minutes, and cook until crispy, flipping halfway through and spraying with oil. Cook in batches if needed.
8. Serve with desired dips and seasonings.

Air fryer Bacon

Prep Time:	10 minutes	Calories:	177
Cook Time:	7 minutes	Fat (g):	17
Total Time:	17 minutes	Protein (g):	5.5
Servings:	4	Carbs (g):	0.4

Ingredients:

- Bacon slices   6 oz

Instructions:

1. Switch on the air fryer, insert the fryer basket, grease it with oil, then set the cooking temperature to 400 degrees F (204 °C) and set frying time for 5 minutes or more to preheat the fryer until the food is ready to cook.
2. Place bacon slices into the fryer basket in a single layer, then set the cooking temperature to 400 degrees F (204 °C), adjust frying time for 7 minutes (if you like crispier, set time for 9-10 minutes), and cook until crispy.
3. When done, transfer bacon slices to the paper towel.
4. Serve with desired dips and seasonings.

Air fryer Potato Chips

Prep Time:	15 minutes	Calories:	154
Cook Time:	25 minutes	Fat (g):	3
Total Time:	40 minutes	Protein (g):	5
Servings:	4	Carbs (g):	26

Ingredients:

- Potatoes, medium   4
- Olive oil   1 tablespoon
- Salt   To taste

Instructions:

1. Switch on the air fryer, insert the fryer basket, grease it with oil, then set the cooking temperature to 400 degrees F (204 °C) and set frying time for 5 minutes or more to preheat the fryer until the food is ready to cook.
2. Meanwhile, slice the potatoes into thin slices. Place the sliced potato into a large bowl with cold water and let it soak for about 20 minutes.
3. When done, pat dry them with a paper towel. Season the sliced potato with oil and salt.
4. Place the potato chips into the fryer basket, then set the cooking temperature to 200 degrees F (93 °C), adjust frying time for 20 minutes, and cook.
5. When done, toss the chips and then set the cooking temperature to 400 degrees F (204 °C), adjust frying time for 5-7 minutes, and cook until crispy.
6. Serve with desired dips and seasonings.

Air fryer Asparagus

Prep Time:	5 minutes	Calories:	110
Cook Time:	10 minutes	Fat (g):	2.6
Total Time:	15 minutes	Protein (g):	10
Servings:	2	Carbs (g):	12.5

Ingredients:

- Asparagus — 1 bundle
- Olive oil — 1 teaspoon
- Garlic salt — 1/8 teaspoon
- Parmesan cheese, grated — 1 tablespoon
- Black pepper — To taste

Instructions:

1. Switch on the air fryer, insert the fryer basket, grease it with oil, then set the cooking temperature to 400 degrees F (204 °C) and set frying time for 5 minutes or more to preheat the fryer until the food is ready to cook.
2. Place the asparagus into the fryer basket in a single layer, and drizzle with oil. Sprinkle salt, pepper, and cheese on top.
3. Set cooking temperature to 400 degrees F (204 °C), adjust frying time for 10 minutes, and cook, flipping halfway through and spraying with oil.
4. Serve with desired dips and seasonings.

Air fryer Scotch Eggs

Prep Time:	10 minutes	Calories:	323
Cook Time:	15 minutes	Fat (g):	26
Total Time:	25 minutes	Protein (g):	20
Servings:	6	Carbs (g):	3

Ingredients:

- Bulk sausage
- Eggs, boiled, peeled
- Eggs, raw
- All-purpose flour
- Salt

1 lb (453g)

6

2

½ cup

1 teaspoon

- Thyme   ½ teaspoon
- Black pepper   1 teaspoon
- Garlic cloves, minced   2
- Paprika   ½ teaspoon
- Onion, chopped   1/3 cup

Instructions:

1. Switch on the air fryer, insert the fryer basket, grease it with oil, then set the cooking temperature to 400 degrees F (204 °C) and set frying time for 5 minutes or more to preheat the fryer until the food is ready to cook.
2. In a medium bowl, mix sausage, garlic, thyme, onion, ½ teaspoon of salt and pepper, and mix well.
3. In another medium bowl, mix flour, paprika, and remaining salt and pepper, and mix well.
4. Take a small bowl, crack 2 raw eggs in it and whisk well and set aside.
5. Meanwhile, divide the sausage mixture into six portions. Wrap the sausage around each boiled egg.
6. Dredge each egg in the flour mixture and then dip into the raw egg mixture.
7. Place scotch eggs into the fryer basket in a single layer, then set the cooking temperature to 400 degrees F (204 °C), adjust frying time for 15 minutes, and cook, flipping halfway through and spraying with oil.
8. Serve with desired dips and seasonings.

Air fryer Shrimp Scampi

Prep Time:	5 minutes	Calories:	215
Cook Time:	7 minutes	Fat (g):	12
Total Time:	12 minutes	Protein (g):	23
Servings:	4	Carbs (g):	1

Ingredients:

• Shrimp, raw, peeled and deveined	1 lb (453g)
• Butter	4 tablespoons
• Minced garlic	1 tablespoon
• Lemon juice	1 tablespoon
• Red pepper flakes	1 tablespoon

• Chives, chopped	1 tablespoon
• Basil, chopped	1 tablespoon
• Chicken stock	2 tablespoons

Instructions:

1. Switch on the air fryer, insert the fryer basket, then set the cooking temperature to 400 degrees F (204 °C) and set frying time for 2 minutes or more to preheat the fryer until the food is ready to cook.
2. Meanwhile, take a 6-inch baking pan. Add in butter, garlic, and pepper flakes. Place the pan into the air fryer and cook for about 2 minutes.
3. When done, add all the remaining ingredients into the pan and mix well.
4. Set cooking temperature to 350 degrees F (177 °C), adjust frying time for 5 minutes, and cook, stirring once.
5. When done, remove the baking pan and place it onto a wire rack, mix well and let it rest for 1 minute.
6. Serve.

Air fryer Fish

Prep Time:	5 minutes	Calories:	162
Cook Time:	13 minutes	Fat (g):	4
Total Time:	18 minutes	Protein (g):	21
Servings:	8	Carbs (g):	11

Ingredients:

- Fish fillets   8
- Olive oil   2 tablespoons
- Paprika   ½ teaspoon
- Chili powder   ¼ teaspoon
- Breadcrumbs   1 cup

- Salt   ½ teaspoon
- Black pepper   ¼ teaspoon
- Garlic powder   ¼ teaspoon
- Onion powder   ¼ teaspoon

Instructions:

1. Switch on the air fryer, insert the fryer basket, grease it with oil, then set the cooking temperature to 400 degrees F (204 °C) and set frying time for 5 minutes or more to preheat the fryer until the food is ready to cook.
2. Meanwhile, drizzle fillets with olive oil.
3. In a medium bowl, place all the remaining ingredients and mix well.
4. Coat each fish piece with breadcrumbs mixture until evenly covered on all sides.
5. Place fish fillets into the fryer basket in a single layer, then set the cooking temperature to 400 degrees F (204 °C), adjust frying time for 13 minutes, and cook, flipping halfway through. Cook fish fillets in batches if needed.
6. Serve with tartar sauce.

Air fryer Breakfast Frittata

Prep Time:	5 minutes	Calories:	149
Cook Time:	15 minutes	Fat (g):	11
Total Time:	20 minutes	Protein (g):	9
Servings:	4	Carbs (g):	3

Ingredients:

- Eggs, beaten — 4
- Heavy cream — 3 tablespoons
- Cheddar cheese, grated — 4 tablespoons
- Mushrooms, sliced — 4
- Cherry tomatoes, halved — 3

- Spinach, chopped   4 tablespoons
- Green onion, sliced   1
- Salt   To taste
- Parsley, chopped   2 tablespoons

Instructions:

1. Switch on the air fryer, insert the fryer basket, then set the cooking temperature to 400 degrees F (204 °C) and set frying time for 5 minutes or more to preheat the fryer until the food is ready to cook.
2. Meanwhile, take a 7-inch baking pan, line it with parchment paper, and grease it with oil.
3. In a bowl, place eggs and cream and whisk well.
4. Add in all the remaining ingredients and mix well.
5. Pour the egg mixture into the baking pan and place the pan inside the fryer basket.
6. Set cooking temperature to 350 degrees F (177 °C), adjust frying time for 15 minutes, and cook until ready.
7. Serve with desired dips and seasonings.

Air fryer Zucchini Chips

Prep Time:	10 minutes	Calories:	211
Cook Time:	11 minutes	Fat (g):	4
Total Time:	21 minutes	Protein (g):	9
Servings:	4	Carbs (g):	32

Ingredients:

- Zucchini, large, sliced about ¼-inch thick   1
- All-purpose flour   ½ cup
- Paprika   1 teaspoon
- Italian seasoning   1 teaspoon

- Parmesan cheese, grated   ¼ cup
- Eggs   2
- Breadcrumbs   1 ½ cups
- Salt and pepper   To taste

Instructions:

1. Switch on the air fryer, insert the fryer basket, grease it with oil, then set the cooking temperature to 400 degrees F (204 °C) and set frying time for 5 minutes or more to preheat the fryer until the food is ready to cook.
2. Meanwhile, in a medium bowl, add flour, salt, pepper, paprika, Italian seasoning, and cheese.
3. In another bowl, crack the eggs in it and whisk well, and set aside.
4. Add breadcrumbs into the third bowl.
5. Prepare zucchini chips and for this, dredge each zucchini chip in the flour mixture, then dip into beaten egg and finally coat with breadcrumbs.
6. Place zucchini chips into the fryer basket in a single layer, then set the cooking temperature to 400 degrees F (204 °C), adjust frying time for 10-11 minutes, and cook until crispy, flipping halfway through and spraying with oil. Cook chips in batches if needed.
7. Serve with desired dips and seasonings.

Air fryer Roasted Cauliflower

Prep Time:	5 minutes	Calories:	78
Cook Time:	15 minutes	Fat (g):	7
Total Time:	20 minutes	Protein (g):	1
Servings:	4	Carbs (g):	3.7

Ingredients:

- Cauliflower, cut into florets — 1 head
- Olive oil — 4 tablespoons
- Salt — To taste
- Black pepper — To taste

Instructions:

1. Switch on the air fryer, insert the fryer basket, grease it with oil, then set the cooking temperature to 375 degrees F (190 °C) and set frying time for 5 minutes or more to preheat the fryer until the food is ready to cook.
2. Meanwhile, toss cauliflower florets with salt, pepper, and olive oil.
3. Place cauliflower florets into the fryer basket in a single layer, then set the cooking temperature to 375 degrees F (190 °C), adjust frying time for 15 minutes, and cook until slightly browned. Cook cauliflower in batches if needed.
4. Serve with desired dips and seasonings.

Air fryer Brussels Sprouts

Prep Time:	10 minutes	Calories:	139
Cook Time:	15 minutes	Fat (g):	9
Total Time:	25 minutes	Protein (g):	4
Servings:	4	Carbs (g):	13

Ingredients:

- Brussels sprouts, halved — 1 lb (453g)
- Butter, unsalted, melted — 2 tablespoons
- Salt — ½ teaspoon
- Olive oil — 1 tablespoon
- Shallot, medium, chopped — 1
- Red wine vinegar — 1 teaspoon

Instructions:

1. Switch on the air fryer, insert the fryer basket, grease it with oil, then set the cooking temperature to 375 degrees F (190 °C) and set frying time for 5 minutes or more to preheat the fryer until the food is ready to cook.
2. Meanwhile, toss brussels sprouts with salt and olive oil.
3. Place brussels sprouts into the fryer basket in a single layer, then set the cooking temperature to 375 degrees F (190 °C), adjust frying time for 15 minutes, and cook, flipping halfway through and spraying with oil. Cook brussels sprouts in batches if needed.
4. Meanwhile, take a bowl, add in shallot, butter, red wine vinegar, and mix well.
5. When brussels sprouts are ready, transfer them into a bowl and then add in butter mixture. Mix well and serve.

Air fryer Buffalo Chicken Wings

Prep Time:	5 minutes	Calories:	365
Cook Time:	25 minutes	Fat (g):	24
Total Time:	30 minutes	Protein (g):	36
Servings:	4	Carbs (g):	1

Ingredients:

- Chicken wings
- Butter, melted
- Red hot sauce
- Worcestershire sauce
- Tabasco sauce

2 pounds
6 tablespoons
12 oz
¼ teaspoon
¼ teaspoon

Instructions:

1. Switch on the air fryer, insert the fryer basket, grease it with oil, then set the cooking temperature to 400 degrees F (204 °C) and set frying time for 5 minutes or more to preheat the fryer until the food is ready to cook.
2. Place chicken wings into the fryer basket, then set the cooking temperature to 400 degrees F (204 °C), adjust frying time for 25 minutes, and cook until crispy and golden brown, shaking every 5 minutes.
3. Prepare buffalo sauce and for this, place all the remaining ingredients into a bowl.
4. When chicken wings are ready, transfer them into a bowl with buffalo sauce. Toss them well and then serve.

Air fryer Meatloaf

Prep Time:	10 minutes	Calories:	188
Cook Time:	45 minutes	Fat (g):	10
Total Time:	55 minutes	Protein (g):	17
Servings:	12	Carbs (g):	6

Ingredients:

- Ground beef   2 lbs (907g)
- Eggs, beaten   2
- Onion, diced   1 cup
- Garlic cloves, minced   4
- Breadcrumbs   ½ cup
- Butter   1 tablespoon
- Salt and pepper   To taste

- Paprika — ½ teaspoon
- Worcestershire sauce — 2 tablespoons
- Italian seasoning — 1 tablespoon
- Parsley, chopped — 3 tablespoons

Meatloaf Glaze:
- Worcestershire sauce — 1 teaspoon
- Salt — ½ teaspoon
- Pepper — ½ teaspoon
- Garlic powder — 1 teaspoon
- Ketchup — ¾ cup

Instructions:

1. Switch on the air fryer, insert the fryer basket, grease it with oil, then set the cooking temperature to 370 degrees F (188 °C) and set frying time for 5 minutes or more to preheat the fryer until the food is ready to cook.
2. Meanwhile, in a large pan, heat oil, and add butter and onion. Cook for 3 minutes.
3. Take a large bowl, place the cooked onion into it and then add all the remaining ingredients except for the glaze ingredients. Mix well until combined.
4. Take a 9x5 pan and line it with parchment paper. Add meat mixture into it. Shape the mixture in a loaf pan, and smooth with a silicone spatula. Then remove it from the pan with the parchment paper and place the mixture into the fryer basket.
5. Set the cooking temperature to 370 degrees F (188 °C), adjust frying time for 35 minutes, and start cooking.
6. Meanwhile, place all the ingredients for the glaze into a bowl and mix well.
7. After 35 minutes, transfer the meatloaf onto a plate, then spread the glaze over the top of the meat.
8. Continue cooking the meatloaf in the air fryer for 10 minutes.
9. Serve with desired dips and seasonings.

Air fryer Potato Wedges

Prep Time:	15 minutes	Calories:	118
Cook Time:	15 minutes	Fat (g):	3
Total Time:	30 minutes	Protein (g):	2
Servings:	2	Carbs (g):	20

Ingredients:

- Potatoes, cut into wedges   2
- Olive oil   2 tablespoons
- Garlic salt   1 teaspoon
- Rosemary   1 teaspoon
- Parsley   1 teaspoon

- Oregano   ½ teaspoon
- Paprika   ½ teaspoon

Instructions:

1. Switch on the air fryer, insert the fryer basket, grease it with oil, then set the cooking temperature to 400 degrees F (204 °C) and set frying time for 5 minutes or more to preheat the fryer until the food is ready to cook.
2. Meanwhile, place the potato wedges into a large bowl with warm water and let them soak for about 10 minutes.
3. Take a small bowl and mix all the remaining ingredients.
4. Drain the water from the bowl and then season potato wedges with the prepared seasonings.
5. Place potato wedges into the fryer basket in a single layer, then set the cooking temperature to 400 degrees F (204 °C), adjust frying time for 15 minutes, and cook until crispy, flipping halfway through and spraying with oil.
6. Serve with desired dips and seasonings.

Air fryer Baked Potatoes

Prep Time:	10 minutes	Calories:	160
Cook Time:	40 minutes	Fat (g):	1
Total Time:	50 minutes	Protein (g):	4.5
Servings:	2	Carbs (g):	35

Ingredients:

- Russet potatoes, medium, rinsed, dried   2
- Olive oil   1 teaspoon
- Salt   ½ teaspoon + for serving
- Butter   For serving
- Black pepper   For serving

Instructions:

1. Switch on the air fryer, insert the fryer basket, grease it with oil, then set the cooking temperature to 400 degrees F (204 °C) and set frying time for 5 minutes or more to preheat the fryer until the food is ready to cook.
2. Meanwhile, coat the potatoes with olive oil and season with salt.
3. Place potatoes into the fryer basket, then set cooking temperature to 375 degrees F (190°C), adjust frying time for 40 minutes, and cook, flipping halfway through and spraying with oil.
4. When done, transfer potatoes onto a plate, cut them lengthwise.
5. Serve with butter, salt, and black pepper.

Air fryer Fried Okra

Prep Time:	10 minutes	Calories:	114
Cook Time:	10 minutes	Fat (g):	2
Total Time:	20 minutes	Protein (g):	5
Servings:	4	Carbs (g):	20

Ingredients:

- Cornmeal   1 cup
- All-purpose flour   ¼ cup
- Salt   To taste
- Okra, fresh   ½ lb (227g)
- Egg, beaten   1

Instructions:

1. Switch on the air fryer, insert the fryer basket, grease it with oil, then set the cooking temperature to 400 degrees F (204 °C) and set frying time for 5 minutes or more to preheat the fryer until the food is ready to cook.
2. Meanwhile, cut okra into ½-inch slices.
3. Place beaten egg into a small bowl.
4. Place cornmeal, flour, and salt into another bowl.
5. Prepare okra and for this, dip each okra piece into an egg and then coat each piece with the cornmeal mixture until evenly covered on all sides.
6. Place okra into the fryer basket in a single layer, then set the cooking temperature to 400 degrees F (204 °C), adjust frying time for 10 minutes, and cook, shaking after 5 minutes. Cook okra in batches if you needed.
7. Serve with desired dips and seasonings.

Air fryer Chicken Thighs

Prep Time:	5 minutes	Calories:	132
Cook Time:	15 minutes	Fat (g):	4
Total Time:	20 minutes	Protein (g):	20
Servings:	4	Carbs (g):	2

Ingredients:

- Chicken thighs, skinless   4
- Ground ginger   ¼ teaspoon
- Salt   1 teaspoon
- Black pepper   ¼ teaspoon
- Paprika   2 teaspooons
- Garlic powder   2 teaspooons

Instructions:

1. Switch on the air fryer, insert the fryer basket, grease it with oil, then set the cooking temperature to 400 degrees F (204 °C) and set frying time for 5 minutes or more to preheat the fryer until the food is ready to cook.
2. Meanwhile, mix all ingredients except for chicken in a bowl.
3. Season chicken thighs with prepared seasoning until evenly covered on all sides.
4. Place chicken thighs into the fryer basket in a single layer, then set the cooking temperature to 400 degrees F (204 °C), adjust frying time for 15-20 minutes and cook until internal temperature reaches 165 degrees F (74 °C), flipping halfway through and spraying with oil.
5. Serve with desired dips and seasonings.

Air fryer Roasted Chickpeas

Prep Time:	10 minutes	Calories:	185
Cook Time:	15 minutes	Fat (g):	6.7
Total Time:	25 minutes	Protein (g):	7.7
Servings:	4	Carbs (g):	24

Ingredients:

- Chickpeas, canned, rinsed   15 oz (425g)
- Olive oil   2 teaspoons
- Salt   1/4 teaspoon
- Paprika   1/2 teaspoon
- Garlic powder   1/2 teaspoon
- Onion powder   1/4 teaspoon

Instructions:

1. Switch on the air fryer, insert the fryer basket, grease it with oil, then set the cooking temperature to 400 degrees F (204 °C) and set frying time for 5 minutes or more to preheat the fryer until the food is ready to cook.
2. Meanwhile, take a large bowl, then pat dry chickpeas with paper towels and place them into the bowl.
3. Season chickpeas with oil, salt, paprika, garlic and onion powder, and mix well.
4. Place chickpeas into the fryer basket in a single layer, then set the cooking temperature to 400 degrees F (204 °C), adjust frying time for 15 minutes, and cook until crispy, shaking after 10 minutes.
5. Serve with desired dips and seasonings.

Air fryer Sweet Potato Tots

Prep Time:	10 minutes	Calories:	156
Cook Time:	24 minutes	Fat (g):	1
Total Time:	34 minutes	Protein (g):	4
Servings:	4	Carbs (g):	33

Ingredients:

- Sweet potato puree   2 cups
- Coriander   ½ teaspoon
- Cumin   ½ teaspoon
- Salt   ½ teaspoon
- Breadcrumbs   ½ cup

Instructions:

1. Switch on the air fryer, insert the fryer basket, grease it with olive oil, then set the cooking temperature to 400 degrees F (204 °C), and set frying time for 5 minutes or more to preheat the fryer.
2. Meanwhile, take a large bowl, mix all ingredients in it.
3. Take a cookie scoop, form tots from the sweet potato mixture, and then place them on a plate. Spray the tots with oil.
4. Place sweet potato tots into the fryer basket in a single layer, then set the cooking temperature to 400 degrees F (204 °C), adjust frying time for 12 minutes (6 minutes per side), and cook until crispy, flipping halfway through and spraying with oil. Cook tots in batches.
5. Serve with desired dips and seasonings.

Air fryer Crab Cakes

Prep Time:	25 minutes	Calories:	237
Cook Time:	15 minutes	Fat (g):	5
Total Time:	40 minutes	Protein (g):	13
Servings:	4	Carbs (g):	33

Ingredients:

- Onion, diced   1
- Egg   1
- Crabmeat   1 cup
- Breadcrumbs   1 cup
- Worcestershire sauce   1 teaspoon

- Seafood seasoning   1 teaspoon
- Mayonnaise   2 tablespoons
- Dijon mustard   ½ teaspoon
- Salt   ¼ teaspoon
- Panko breadcrumbs   ½ cup

Instructions:

1. Switch on the air fryer, insert the fryer basket, grease it with olive oil, then set the cooking temperature to 350 degrees F (177 °C) and set frying time for 5 minutes or more to preheat the fryer.
2. Meanwhile, take a large bowl, mix all ingredients in it except for panko breadcrumbs.
3. Make the 4 patties from the crab mixture.
4. Dredge each patty in panko breadcrumbs until evenly covered on all sides.
5. Place crab cakes in the refrigerator for 15 minutes.
6. After that, spray crab cakes with oil, and place them into the fryer basket in a single layer, then set the cooking temperature to 350 degrees F (177 °C), adjust frying time for 15 minutes, and cook until crispy, flipping halfway through and spraying with oil.
7. When done, transfer crab cakes onto a plate.
8. Serve with desired dips and seasonings.

Air fryer Meatballs in Tomato Sauce

Prep Time:	10 minutes	Calories:	235
Cook Time:	25 minutes	Fat (g):	13
Total Time:	35 minutes	Protein (g):	16
Servings:	4	Carbs (g):	12

Ingredients:

- Onion, chopped   1
- Ground beef   12 oz (340g)
- Egg   1

- Breadcrumbs — 3 tablespoons
- Salt and pepper — To taste
- Tomato sauce — ¾ cup
- Parsley, chopped — 1 tablespoon
- Thyme leaves, chopped — 1 tablespoon

Instructions:

1. Switch on the air fryer, insert the fryer basket, grease it with olive oil, then set the cooking temperature to 400 degrees F (204 °C), and set frying time for 5 minutes or more to preheat the fryer.
2. Meanwhile, take a large bowl, place all ingredients in it except for tomato sauce, and mix well.
3. Shape the mixture into 12 patties.
4. Place the meatballs into the fryer basket in a single layer, then set the cooking temperature to 400 degrees F (204 °C), adjust frying time for 10 minutes, and cook. Cook meatballs in 2 batches.
5. When done, transfer meatballs into a baking dish. Add tomato sauce and then place the dish into the fryer basket. Set cooking temperature to 350 degrees F (177 °C) and continue cooking for 5 minutes.
6. Serve with desired dips and seasonings.

Air fryer Butternut Squash

Prep Time:	10 minutes	Calories:	58
Cook Time:	20 minutes	Fat (g):	2
Total Time:	30 minutes	Protein (g):	1
Servings:	4	Carbs (g):	11

Ingredients:

- Butternut squash, cubed   4 cups
- Cinnamon   1 teaspoon

Instructions:

1. Switch on the air fryer, insert the fryer basket, grease it with olive oil, then set the cooking temperature to 400 degrees F (204 °C), and set frying time for 5 minutes or more to preheat the fryer.
2. Place the butternut squash into the fryer basket in a single layer, sprinkle with cinnamon, then set the cooking temperature to 400 degrees F (204 °C), adjust frying time for 20 minutes, and cook, flipping halfway through and spraying with oil. Cook the butternut squash in batches if you needed.
3. Serve with desired dips and seasonings.

Air fryer Steak

Prep Time:	5 minutes	Calories:	375
Cook Time:	16 minutes	Fat (g):	26
Total Time:	21 minutes	Protein (g):	34
Servings:	2	Carbs (g):	0

Ingredients:

- Steaks   2 (6 oz each)
- Olive oil   1 teaspoon
- Salt   To taste
- Black pepper   To taste
- Garlic powder   ½ teaspoon

Instructions:

1. Switch on the air fryer, insert the fryer basket, grease it with olive oil, then set the cooking temperature to 400 degrees F (204 °C), and set frying time for 5 minutes or more to preheat the fryer.
2. Meanwhile, season steaks with salt, pepper, and garlic powder. Coat both sides of steaks with olive oil.
3. Place steaks into the fryer basket, then set cooking temperature to 400 degrees F (204 °C), adjust frying time for 16 minutes, and cook, flipping halfway through and spraying with oil.
4. When done, transfer steaks to a plate and serve immediately.

Air fryer BBQ Ribs

Prep Time:	5 minutes	Calories:	472
Cook Time:	43 minutes	Fat (g):	28
Total Time:	48 minutes	Protein (g):	30
Servings:	4	Carbs (g):	25

Ingredients:

- Pork baby back ribs   1 slab
- Onion powder   ½ tablespoon
- Paprika   ½ tablespoon
- Black pepper   ½ tablespoon
- Brown sugar   ¼ cup

- Garlic powder   ½ tablespoon
- Salt   ½ tablespoon
- Red pepper flakes   ½ tablespoon
- Celery seeds   1 teaspoon
- Barbecue sauce   1 cup

Instructions:

1. Switch on the air fryer, insert the fryer basket, grease it with olive oil, then set the cooking temperature to 400 degrees F (204 °C), and set frying time for 5 minutes or more to preheat the fryer.
2. Meanwhile, take a small bowl, add all ingredients except for ribs and barbecue sauce into the bowl and mix until combined.
3. Rub the ribs with the mixture. Slice the ribs in half.
4. Place ribs into the fryer basket, then set the cooking temperature to 400 degrees F (204 °C), adjust frying time for 40 minutes, and cook, flipping halfway through.
5. When done, slice the ribs into small individual ribs. Place ribs in a bowl, add barbecue sauce, and mix well.
6. Set cooking temperature to 400 degrees F (204 °C) and continue cooking for 3 minutes.
7. Serve with desired dips and seasonings.

Air fryer Salmon

Prep Time:	5 minutes	Calories:	437
Cook Time:	12 minutes	Fat (g):	26
Total Time:	17 minutes	Protein (g):	45
Servings:	2	Carbs (g):	4

Ingredients:

- Salmon fillet
- Butter
- Lemon
- Garlic salt

1 pound (453 g)
2 tablespoons
½
To taste

Instructions:

1. Switch on the air fryer, insert the fryer basket, grease it with olive oil, then set the cooking temperature to 400 degrees F (204 °C), and set frying time for 5 minutes or more to preheat the fryer.
2. Meanwhile, season salmon with garlic salt.
3. Place salmon fillet into the fryer basket. Top with butter and lemon slices.
4. Set the cooking temperature to 400 degrees F (204 °C), adjust frying time for 12 minutes, and cook until the internal temperature reaches 145 degrees F (63 °C).
5. Serve with desired dips and seasonings.

Air fryer General Tso's Chicken

Prep Time:	10 minutes	Calories:	399
Cook Time:	15 minutes	Fat (g):	10
Total Time:	25 minutes	Protein (g):	46
Servings:	2	Carbs (g):	29

Ingredients:

- Chicken thighs, skinless, boneless   1 lb (453 g)
- Cornstarch   2 tablespoons
- Black pepper   ½ teaspoon
- Salt   ½ teaspoon
  <u>For the sauce:</u>

- Ketchup   ¼ cup
- Soy sauce   2 tablespoons
- Brown sugar   2 tablespoons
- Ginger paste   ½ teaspoon
- Garlic cloves, crushed   2
- Red pepper flakes   ½ teaspoon

Instructions:

1. Switch on the air fryer, insert the fryer basket, grease it with olive oil, then set the cooking temperature to 400 degrees F (204 °C), and set frying time for 5 minutes or more to preheat the fryer.
2. Meanwhile, cut chicken thighs into small pieces.
3. Toss chicken pieces with salt, pepper, and cornstarch.
4. Place chicken pieces into the fryer basket in a single layer, then set the cooking temperature to 400 degrees F (204 °C), adjust frying time for 10 minutes, and cook until crispy and golden brown, flipping halfway through and spraying with oil.
5. Meanwhile, take a saucepan, place all sauce ingredients in it.
6. Bring to a boil and then simmer for 5 minutes until the sauce has thickened.
7. When done, pour the sauce over the prepared chicken and mix well.
8. Serve with desired dips and seasonings.

Air fryer Whole Chicken

Prep Time:	5 minutes	Calories:	446
Cook Time:	55 minutes	Fat (g):	32
Total Time:	1 hour	Protein (g):	36
Servings:	4	Carbs (g):	1

Ingredients:

- Whole chicken   3 ½ pounds (g)
- Olive oil   2 tablespoons
- Chicken seasoning   1 tablespoon

Instructions:

1. Switch on the air fryer, insert the fryer basket, grease it with olive oil, then set the cooking temperature to 400 degrees F (204 °C), and set frying time for 5 minutes or more to preheat the fryer.
2. Meanwhile, rub the chicken with olive oil and chicken seasoning.
3. Place chicken into the fryer basket, then set the cooking temperature to 350 degrees F (177 °C), adjust frying time for 55 minutes, and cook until crispy and golden brown, flipping halfway through and spraying with oil.
4. Serve with desired dips and seasonings.

Air fryer Bacon Wrapped Avocado

Prep Time:	5 minutes	Calories:	281
Cook Time:	28 minutes	Fat (g):	25
Total Time:	33 minutes	Protein (g):	11.5
Servings:	4	Carbs (g):	1.2

Ingredients:

- Avocados, pitted, peeled, sliced in half   2
- Bacon slices   16

Instructions:

1. Switch on the air fryer, insert the fryer basket, grease it with olive oil, then set the cooking temperature to 400 degrees F (204 °C), and set frying time for 5 minutes or more to preheat the fryer.
2. Meanwhile, slice the avocado halves into 4 pieces.
3. Wrap each avocado slice with a bacon slice.
4. Place avocado-bacon slices into the fryer basket in a single layer, then set the cooking temperature to 400 degrees F (204 °C), adjust frying time for 7 minutes, and cook. Cook avocado-bacon slices in batches.
5. Serve with desired dips and seasonings.

Air fryer Bacon-Wrapped Scallops

Prep Time:	10 minutes	Calories:	223
Cook Time:	14 minutes	Fat (g):	15
Total Time:	24 minutes	Protein (g):	17
Servings:	9	Carbs (g):	3

Ingredients:

- Bay scallops   1 lb (453 g) (36 scallops)
- Sriracha sauce   2 tablespoons
- Mayonnaise   ½ cup
- Bacon slices, cut into thirds   12
- Salt   A pinch
- Black pepper   A pinch

Instructions:

1. Switch on the air fryer, insert the fryer basket, grease it with olive oil, then set the cooking temperature to 400 degrees F (204 °C), and set frying time for 5 minutes or more to preheat the fryer.
2. Meanwhile, take a large bowl, then pat dry scallops with paper towels and place them into the bowl.
3. Season scallops with salt and pepper.
4. Wrap scallops with slices of bacon and secure with a toothpick.
5. Place scallops into the fryer basket in a single layer, then set the cooking temperature to 400 degrees F (204 °C), adjust frying time for 7 minutes, and cook until crispy, flipping halfway through. Cook scallops in batches if you needed.
6. Meanwhile, take a small bowl, and mix Sriracha sauce and mayonnaise in it.
7. When done, serve scallops with Sriracha-mayonnaise sauce.

Air fryer Ratatouille

Prep Time:	15 minutes	Calories:	162
Cook Time:	30 minutes	Fat (g):	8
Total Time:	45 minutes	Protein (g):	4
Servings:	2	Carbs (g):	21

Ingredients:

- Eggplant, cut into cubes   ½
- Zucchini, cut into cubes   1
- Tomato, chopped   1
- Onion, chopped   ½
- Yellow bell pepper, chopped   ½

- Red bell pepper, chopped — ½
- Cayenne pepper, diced — 1
- Garlic clove, crushed — 1
- Olive oil — 1 tablespoon
- Salt and pepper — To taste
- White wine — 1 tablespoon
- Vinegar — 1 teaspoon
- Sprigs fresh basil, chopped — 5
- Sprigs fresh oregano, chopped — 2

Instructions:

1. Switch on the air fryer, insert the fryer basket, then set cooking temperature to 400 degrees F (204 °C), and set frying time for 5 minutes or more to preheat the fryer.
2. Meanwhile, take a large bowl, add all ingredients into it and mix well.
3. Take a baking dish and place vegetable mixture into it.
4. Place the baking dish into the fryer basket, then set the cooking temperature to 400 degrees F (204 °C), adjust frying time for 30 minutes, and cook, stirring every 5 minutes.
5. Serve with desired dips and seasonings.

Air fryer Beef Empanadas

Prep Time:	30 minutes	Calories:	209
Cook Time:	17 minutes	Fat (g):	13
Total Time:	47 minutes	Protein (g):	6
Servings:	8	Carbs (g):	17.7

Ingredients:

- Puff pastry dough   1 package
- Canola oil   1 tablespoon
- Ground beef   ¼ lb (113g)
- White onion, chopped   ¼ cup
- Red bell pepper, seeded and chopped   ¼ cup
- Dried oregano   ¼ teaspoon
- Ground cumin   1 teaspoon

- Sweet paprika   ½ teaspoon
- Salt and ground black pepper   To taste
- Egg   1
- Water   1 tablespoon
- Cooking spray

Instructions:

1. Place the puff pastry dough at room temperature for about 15 minutes before using.
2. In a non-stick skillet, heat the oil over medium-high heat and cook the beef and onion for about 3 minutes, crumbling the meat with a wooden spoon.
3. Stir in the bell pepper and cook for about 4 minutes, stirring occasionally.
4. Stir in the oregano and spices and remove the skillet from the heat.
5. Set aside to cool for about 5 minutes.
6. Cut the puff pastry into 8 (6-inch) rounds and arrange it onto a smooth surface.
7. Place about 1-2 tablespoons of beef mixture in the center of each pastry round.
8. With wet fingers, moisten the outer edges of each round.
9. Then fold round over the filling, and pinch the edges to seal.
10. With a fork, crimp the edges.
11. Set the temperature of the air fryer to 400 degrees F (204 °C) to preheat.
12. For the egg wash: in a bowl, add egg and water and beat well.
13. Brush each empanada with egg wash and then spray with cooking spray lightly.
14. After preheating, place empanadas into the fryer basket in a single layer, then set the cooking temperature to 400 degrees F (204 °C), adjust frying time for 10 minutes, and cook until crispy flipping halfway through.
15. When cooking time is completed, remove the empanadas and serve warm.

Tip:

Use a biscuit cutter to cut the pastry in uniform circles.

Air fryer Salmon Patties

Prep Time:	15 minutes	Calories:	348
Cook Time:	13 minutes	Fat (g):	29.9
Total Time:	28 minutes	Protein (g):	15.6
Servings:	4	Carbs (g):	6.1

Ingredients:

Dipping Sauce:

- Mayonnaise   ½ cup
- Lemon juice   ½ teaspoon
- Garlic, minced   1 teaspoon
- Cajun seasoning   2 pinches

For Patties:

- Canned salmon, minced — 12 oz (340g)
- Garlic, minced — 1 teaspoon
- Fresh chives, chopped — 1 tablespoon
- Dried parsley — 1 teaspoon
- Salt — ½ teaspoon
- All-purpose flour — 1 ½ tablespoon
- Lemon slices — 4
- Cooking spray

Instructions:

1. Switch on the air fryer, insert the fryer basket, grease it with cooking spray, then set cooking temperature to 350 degrees F (177 °C) and set frying time for 5 minutes or more to preheat the fryer.
2. For the dipping sauce: in a bowl, place all ingredients and mix until well combined.
3. Refrigerate until using.
4. For patties: in a bowl, add salmon, garlic, chives, parsley, and salt and mix well.
5. Add flour and mix until well combined.
6. Make 4 equal-sized patties from the mixture.
7. After preheating, arrange the lemon slices into the greased air fryer basket.
8. Place the patties on top of lemon slices and slide the basket into the air fryer.
9. Immediately set the temperature of the air fryer to 275 degrees F (135 °C) and set the time for 10-13 minutes and cook until crispy.
10. When cooking time is completed, remove the patties and serve alongside the dipping sauce.

Tip:

You can also use cooked salmon instead of canned salmon.

Air fryer Coconut Shrimp

Prep Time:	15 minutes	Calories:	283
Cook Time:	9 minutes	Fat (g):	10.8
Total Time:	24 minutes	Protein (g):	26.5
Servings:	4	Carbs (g):	16.5

Ingredients:

- Shrimp, peeled and deveined   1 lb (453g)
- All-purpose flour   ½ cup
- Eggs, beaten   2

- Unsweetened coconut, shredded   ½ cup
- Panko breadcrumbs   ¼ cup
- Salt   1 teaspoon
- Ground black pepper   ¼ teaspoon
- Olive oil for spraying

Instructions:

1. Switch on the air fryer, insert the fryer basket, grease it with olive oil, then set the cooking temperature to 400 degrees F (204 °C), and set frying time for 5 minutes or more to preheat the fryer.
2. In a shallow bowl, place the flour.
3. In a second shallow bowl, crack the egg and beat slightly.
4. In a third shallow bowl, mix the coconut, breadcrumbs, salt, and black pepper.
5. Dredge each shrimp in flour, then dip into beaten egg and finally coat with coconut mixture.
6. Arrange the shrimp into the greased air fryer basket in a single layer and spray with cooking spray lightly.
7. Slide the basket into the air fryer and set the time for 9 minutes.
8. After 4 minutes of cooking, flip the shrimp and spray with cooking spray lightly.
9. When cooking time is completed, remove the shrimp and serve alongside your favorite dipping sauce.

Tip:

Make sure to pat dry the shrimp thoroughly before coating.

Air fryer Hash Brown

Prep Time:	40 minutes	Calories:	267
Cook Time:	35 minutes	Fat (g):	2.4
Total Time:	1 h 15 m	Protein (g):	7
Servings:	4	Carbs (g):	54

Ingredients:

- Russet potatoes, large, peeled, and shredded 4
- Breadcrumbs 2 tablespoons

- Onion powder   1 teaspoon
- Garlic powder   1 teaspoon
- Salt, divided   2 teaspoons
- Ground black pepper   1 teaspoon

Instructions:

1. In a bowl of cold water, soak the shredded potatoes and set aside for about 15-20 minutes.
2. Drain the potatoes through a colander and rinse under cold running water.
3. In a microwave-safe bowl, place the shredded potatoes and microwave on high for about 4-5 minutes, stirring every 1 minute.
4. Remove from the microwave and place the potatoes onto a paper towel-lined baking sheet.
5. With more paper towels, pat dry the potatoes completely.
6. In a bowl, place the potatoes, breadcrumbs, onion powder, garlic powder, 1 teaspoon of salt, and black pepper and mix until well combined.
7. With a spoon, place the potato mixture onto a parchment paper-lined baking sheet and then shape each into a patty.
8. Refrigerate the hash browns for about 15 minutes.
9. Switch on the air fryer, insert the fryer basket, grease it with olive oil, then set the cooking temperature to 360 degrees F (182 °C) and set frying time for 10 minutes or more to preheat the fryer.
10. After preheating, arrange the hash browns into the greased air fryer basket in batches.
11. Slide the basket into the air fryer and set the time for 15 minutes.
12. Flip the hash browns once halfway through.
13. When cooking time is completed, remove the hash browns and transfer them onto a platter.
14. Sprinkle with the remaining salt and serve immediately.

Air fryer Avocado Fries

Prep Time:	15 minutes	Calories:	275
Cook Time:	7 minutes	Fat (g):	18.5
Total Time:	22 minutes	Protein (g):	5
Servings:	4	Carbs (g):	23.6

Ingredients:

For Fries:

- All-purpose flour   ½ cup
- Ground black pepper   1 ½ teaspoons
- Eggs, large, beaten   2

- Water   1 tablespoon
- Panko breadcrumbs   ½ cup
- Avocados, peeled, pitted, and cut each   2
  into 8 wedges
- Salt   ¼ teaspoon
- Cooking spray

For Dipping Sauce:
- Ketchup   ¼ cup
- Mayonnaise   2 tablespoons
- Sriracha   1 tablespoon
- Apple cider vinegar   1 tablespoon

Instructions:

1. In a shallow dish, mix the flour and black pepper.
2. In a second shallow dish, add the eggs and water, and beat lightly.
3. In a third shallow dish, place the breadcrumbs.
4. Coat avocado wedges with flour mixture, then dip into beaten egg and finally coat with breadcrumbs.
5. Spray the avocado wedges with cooking spray generously.
6. Switch on the air fryer, insert the fryer basket, grease it with olive oil, then set the cooking temperature to 400 degrees F (204 °C), and set frying time for 5 minutes or more to preheat the fryer.
7. After preheating, arrange the avocado wedges into the greased air fryer basket in a single layer.
8. Slide the basket into the air fryer and set the time for 7 minutes.
9. Flip the avocado wedges once halfway through.
10. Meanwhile, for dipping sauce: in a bowl, add all ingredients and beat until well combined.
11. When cooking time is completed, remove the avocado fries and transfer them onto a platter.
12. Sprinkle with the salt and serve immediately alongside the dipping sauce.

Air fryer Chicken Quesadillas

Prep Time:	20 minutes	Calories:	268
Cook Time:	10 minutes	Fat (g):	9
Total Time:	30 minutes	Protein (g):	31.3
Servings:	2	Carbs (g):	13.5

Ingredients:

- Cooked chicken   1/3 cup
- Ground cumin   1/8 teaspoon
- Red chili powder   1/8 teaspoon
- Tortillas, 6-inch   2

- Cheddar cheese, shredded   1/3 cup
- Mozzarella cheese, shredded   ½ cup
- Scallions, chopped   1 tablespoon
- Spinach leaves, chopped   5
- Cooking spray

Instructions:

1. In a small bowl, add chicken, cumin, and chili powder and mix well.
2. Spray 1 side of tortilla with cooking spray.
3. Arrange tortilla onto a smooth surface, greased side down.
4. Place cheddar cheese over the tortilla, followed by the chicken, scallions, spinach, and mozzarella cheese.
5. Cover with the remaining tortilla and spray the top with cooking spray.
6. Switch on the air fryer, insert the fryer basket, grease it with olive oil, then set the cooking temperature to 370 degrees F (188 °C) and set frying time for 5 minutes or more to preheat the fryer.
7. After preheating, arrange the quesadilla into the greased air fryer basket.
8. Slide the basket into the air fryer and set the time for 10 minutes.
9. When cooking time is completed, remove the quesadilla and place it onto a platter.
10. Cut into wedges and serve.

Tip:

Feel free to use greens of your choice.

Air fryer Pork Chops

Prep Time:	10 minutes	Calories:	422
Cook Time:	12 minutes	Fat (g):	26
Total Time:	22 minutes	Protein (g):	43
Servings:	4	Carbs (g):	2

Ingredients:

- Parmesan cheese, grated freshly   ½ cup
- Italian dried herbs   ½ teaspoon
- Ground mustard   1 teaspoon
- Garlic powder   2 teaspoons

- Onion powder   1 teaspoon
- Smoked paprika   1 teaspoon
- Salt   1 teaspoon
- Ground black pepper   ½ teaspoon
- Olive oil   2 tablespoons
- Pork chops, bone-in   4

Instructions:

1. Switch on the air fryer, insert the fryer basket, grease it with olive oil, then set the cooking temperature to 400 degrees F (204 °C), and set frying time for 5 minutes or more to preheat the fryer.
2. In a bowl, place cheese, herbs, mustard, and spices and mix well.
3. Brush the chops evenly with olive oil and then coat with cheese mixture generously.
4. After preheating, arrange the pork chops into the greased air fryer basket.
5. Slide the basket into the air fryer and set the time for 12 minutes.
6. Flip the pork chops once halfway through.
7. When cooking time is completed, remove the pork chops and place them on a platter. Let them rest for about 10 minutes before serving.

Tip:

Make sure to pat dry the pork chops completely before seasoning.

Air fryer Corn on the Cob

Prep Time:	10 minutes	Calories:	179
Cook Time:	10 minutes	Fat (g):	12
Total Time:	20 minutes	Protein (g):	3
Servings:	4	Carbs (g):	17

Ingredients:

- Ears of corn, husked and trimmed   4
- Salt and black pepper   To taste
- Butter, melted   4 teaspoons
- Cooking spray

Instructions:

1. Switch on the air fryer, insert the fryer basket, grease it with olive oil, then set the cooking temperature to 400 degrees F (204 °C), and set frying time for 5 minutes or more to preheat the fryer.
2. Spray ears of corn with cooking spray evenly and then sprinkle with salt and black pepper.
3. After preheating, arrange the ears of corn into the greased air fryer basket.
4. Slide the basket into the air fryer and set the time for 10 minutes.
5. Flip the ears of corn once halfway through.
6. When done, remove the ears of corn and place them onto a platter.
7. Drizzle with melted butter and serve.

Tip:

For a dairy-free version, use coconut milk instead of butter.

Air fryer Spanakopita Bites

Prep Time:	20 minutes	Calories:	85
Cook Time:	24 minutes	Fat (g):	4
Total Time:	44 minutes	Protein (g):	5.2
Servings:	8	Carbs (g):	7

Ingredients:

- Fresh baby spinach leaves   10 oz (283g)
- Water   2 tablespoons
- Egg white   1
- Cottage cheese, 1% low-fat   ¼ cup
- Feta cheese, crumbled   ¼ cup
- Parmesan cheese, grated finely   2 tablespoons
- Lemon zest, grated   1 teaspoon

- Dried oregano — 1 teaspoon
- Salt — ¼ teaspoon
- Ground black pepper — ¼ teaspoon
- Cayenne pepper — 1/8 teaspoon
- Frozen phyllo dough sheets, thawed, (13-x18-inch) — 4
- Olive oil — 1 tablespoon
- Cooking spray

Instructions:

1. In a saucepan, add spinach and water and cook over high heat for about 5 minutes, stirring occasionally.
2. Remove from the heat and drain the spinach completely.
3. Set aside to cool for about 10 minutes.
4. Place the spinach over a paper towel and press firmly to remove the moisture.
5. Place the spinach, egg white, cottage cheese, feta cheese, Parmesan cheese, lemon zest, oregano, salt, black pepper, and cayenne pepper in a bowl, and mix until well combined.
6. Arrange 1 phyllo sheet onto a smooth surface.
7. With a pastry brush, brush the phyllo sheet with oil lightly.
8. Top with the second sheet of phyllo and brush with oil.
9. Repeat the layers.
10. Starting from the long side, cut the stack of phyllo sheets into 8 (2¼-inch wide) strips.
11. Cut each strip in half, crosswise, to form 16 (2¼-inch wide) strips.
12. Place about 1 tablespoon of filling onto the short end of each strip.
13. Fold one corner over the filling to create a triangle.
14. Then fold back and forth to the end of the strip, creating a triangle-shaped phyllo packet.
15. Switch on the air fryer, insert the fryer basket, grease it with olive oil, then set the cooking temperature to 375 degrees F (190 °C), and set frying time for 5 minutes or more to preheat the fryer.
16. After preheating, arrange the packets into the greased air fryer basket in 2 batches and spray with cooking spray lightly.
17. Slide the basket into the air fryer and set the time for 12 minutes.
18. Flip the packets once halfway through.
19. When cooking time is completed, remove the packets and serve warm.

Air fryer Falafel

Prep Time:	15 minutes	Calories:	111
Cook Time:	30 minutes	Fat (g):	2
Total Time:	45 minutes	Protein (g):	6
Servings:	16	Carbs (g):	18

Ingredients:

- Dried chickpeas, soaked   2 cups
- Onion, chopped   1
- Fresh parsley leaves, chopped   1 cup
- Fresh cilantro leaves, chopped   1 cup
- Garlic cloves, minced   3
- Chickpea flour   2 tablespoons
- Ground cumin   2 teaspoons

- Ground coriander — 2 teaspoons
- Sea salt — 1 teaspoon (to taste)
- Ground black pepper — 1 teaspoon
- Cayenne pepper — ½ teaspoon

Instructions:

1. In a food processor, add all the ingredients and pulse until a coarse mixture is formed.
2. Transfer the mixture into a bowl.
3. With your hands, make equal-sized balls from the mixture.
4. Switch on the air fryer, insert the fryer basket, grease it with olive oil, then set the cooking temperature to 375 degrees F (190 °C), and set frying time for 5 minutes or more to preheat the fryer.
5. After preheating, arrange the falafel balls into the greased air fryer basket in 2 batches.
6. Slide the basket into the air fryer and set the time for 15 minutes.
7. Flip the falafel balls once halfway through.
8. When cooking time is completed, remove the falafel balls and serve.

Tip:

Do not over-pulse the mixture.

Air fryer Apple Chips

Prep Time:	10 minutes	Calories:	97
Cook Time:	16 minutes	Fat (g):	1
Total Time:	26 minutes	Protein (g):	1
Servings:	2	Carbs (g):	26

Ingredients:

- Medium Honeycrisp apples, cored and thinly sliced   2

Instructions:

1. Set the temperature of the air fryer to 300 degrees F (149 °C) to preheat.
2. After preheating, arrange the apple slices into the air fryer basket.
3. Cover the apple slices with a metal rack.
4. Slide the basket into the air fryer and set the time for 16 minutes.
5. Flip the apple slices every 5 minutes.
6. When cooking time is completed, remove the apple chips and set them aside to cool for about 5-10 minutes before serving.

Tip:

You can sprinkle these chips with cinnamon.

Air fryer Churro Bites

Prep Time:	1 h 15 m	Calories:	206
Cook Time:	24 minutes	Fat (g):	9
Total Time:	1 h 39 m	Protein (g):	3
Servings:	8	Carbs (g):	27

Ingredients:

- Water — 1 cup
- Granulated sugar, divided — ½ cup + 2 tablespoons
- Unsalted butter, cubed — 1/3 cup
- Salt — ¼ teaspoon
- All-purpose flour — 1 cup
- Large eggs — 2
- Vanilla extract — 1 teaspoon

- Ground cinnamon   ¾ teaspoon
- Cooking spray

Instructions:

1. Line a baking sheet with a greased silicone baking mat.
2. In a medium saucepan, add water, 2 tablespoons of sugar, butter, salt over medium-high heat and bring to a boil.
3. Reduce the heat to medium-low and add the flour, stirring continuously until a smooth dough comes together.
4. Remove from heat and transfer the dough into a bowl.
5. Set aside to cool for about 4 minutes.
6. Add the eggs and vanilla extract into the bowl with dough, and mix with an electric hand mixer, until the dough comes together.
7. With your hands, press the dough to shape into a ball.
8. Transfer the dough into a large piping bag fitted with a large star-shaped tip.
9. Pipe the churros onto the prepared baking sheet into 4-inch lengths.
10. Refrigerate the churros for about 1 hour.
11. After 55 minutes, switch on the air fryer, insert the fryer basket, grease it with olive oil, then set the cooking temperature to 375 degrees F (190 °C), and set frying time for 5 minutes or more to preheat the fryer.
12. After preheating, arrange the churros in 2 batches into the greased air fryer basket, leaving about ½-inch space.
13. Spray the churros with cooking spray evenly.
14. Slide the basket into the air fryer and set the time for 10-12 minutes.
15. Meanwhile, in a shallow bowl, mix the remaining granulated sugar and cinnamon.
16. When cooking time is completed, remove the churros.
17. Immediately transfer the churros into the bowl of sugar mixture and toss to coat well.
18. Serve warm.

Air fryer Doughnuts

Prep Time:	2 h 23 m	Calories:	348
Cook Time:	10 minutes	Fat (g):	10
Total Time:	2 h 33 m	Protein (g):	5
Servings:	8	Carbs (g):	59

Ingredients:

For Doughnuts:
- Milk, warm — 2/3 cup
- Granulated sugar — 3 tablespoons
- Active dry yeast — 1 ½ teaspoons
- All-purpose flour, divided — 2 cups
- Large egg — 1
- Butter, melted — 3 tablespoons
- Vanilla extract — 1 teaspoon
- Salt — ½ teaspoon

For Glaze:

- Confectioners' sugar, sifted — 2 cups
- Butter, melted — 3 tablespoons
- Hot water — 2 ½ tablespoons
- Vanilla extract — 1 teaspoon

Instructions:

1. For the doughnuts: in a bowl, add the milk, sugar, and yeast and mix well.
2. Set aside for about 5-10 minutes.
3. Add about half of the flour, egg, butter, vanilla, and salt and beat until well combined.
4. Set aside for about 5 minutes.
5. Place the dough onto a floured surface and with your hands, knead for about 7-8 minutes.
6. Place the dough into a greased bowl and turn to coat evenly.
7. With plastic wrap, cover the bowl and set aside for about 1-1½ hours or until it doubled in size.
8. Remove the plastic wrap, and with your hands, punch down the dough.
9. Place the dough onto a lightly floured surface and roll into the ¼-3/8-inch thickness
10. With an around 2½-3½-inch cutter, cut the dough.
11. With a small, round cutter cut the hole from the center of each dough round.
12. Arrange the doughnuts onto lightly floured parchment paper and cover them with a kitchen towel.
13. Set aside for about 30 minutes.
14. Switch on the air fryer, insert the fryer basket, grease it with olive oil, then set the cooking temperature to 350 degrees F (177 °C), and set frying time for 5 minutes or more to preheat the fryer.
15. After preheating, arrange the doughnuts into the greased air fryer basket in 2 batches.
16. Slide the basket into the air fryer and set the time for 5-6 minutes.
17. Meanwhile, for glaze: in a bowl, add all ingredients and mix until well combined.
18. When cooking time is completed, remove the doughnuts.
19. Carefully dip the top of each doughnut into the glaze, place it onto a rack, and let it stand until the glaze is set.

Tip:

For golden-brown doughnuts, you can brush them with some melted butter just before placing them into the air fryer.

Air fryer Sweet Potato Chips

Prep Time:	10 minutes	Calories:	130
Cook Time:	30 minutes	Fat (g):	7.1
Total Time:	40 minutes	Protein (g):	1.5
Servings:	2	Carbs (g):	15.5

Ingredients:

- Medium sweet potato, cut into 1/8-inch-thick slices   1
- Canola oil   1 tablespoon
- Sea salt   ¼ teaspoon
- Ground black pepper   ¼ teaspoon
- Cooking spray

Instructions:

1. In a large bowl of cold water, place the sweet potato slices for about 20 minutes.
2. Drain the sweet potato slices, and with paper towels, pat dry them.
3. In a large dry bowl, add the sweet potatoes slices, oil, salt, and black pepper and gently toss to coat.
4. Switch on the air fryer, insert the fryer basket, grease it with olive oil, then set the cooking temperature to 350 degrees F (177 °C), and set frying time for 5 minutes or more to preheat the fryer.
5. After preheating, arrange the sweet potato slices into the greased air fryer basket in 2 batches.
6. Slide the basket into the air fryer and set the time for 15 minutes.
7. When cooking time is completed, remove the sweet potato chips and set them aside to cool before serving.

Tip:

You can use seasoning of your choice.

Air fryer French Toast Sticks

Prep Time:	10 minutes	Calories:	221
Cook Time:	5 minutes	Fat (g):	6.7
Total Time:	15 minutes	Protein (g):	10.4
Servings:	2	Carbs (g):	28.4

Ingredients:

- Bread slices, thick   4
- Milk   ¼ cup
- Eggs   2
- Vanilla extract   1 teaspoon
- Ground nutmeg   1/8 teaspoon
- Ground cinnamon   1 teaspoon

Instructions:

1. Cut each bread slice into thirds to make sticks.
2. In a bowl, add the milk, eggs, vanilla extract, cinnamon, and nutmeg and beat until well combined.
3. Dip each breadstick into the egg mixture evenly.
4. Shake each breadstick to remove excess liquid.
5. Switch on the air fryer, insert the fryer basket, grease it with olive oil, then set the cooking temperature to 360 degrees F (182 °C), and set frying time for 5 minutes or more to preheat the fryer.
6. After preheating, arrange the breadsticks into the parchment paper-lined air fryer basket.
7. Slide the basket into the air fryer and set the time for 5 minutes.
8. When cooking time is completed, remove the French toast sticks and serve.

Tip:

For a sweeter version, you can add a sweetener of your choice into the egg mixture.

Air fryer Eggplant Fries

Prep Time:	15 minutes	Calories:	183
Cook Time:	15 minutes	Fat (g):	5.2
Total Time:	30 minutes	Protein (g):	9.3
Servings:	4	Carbs (g):	25.6

Ingredients:

- Eggplant, medium   1
- All-purpose flour   ¼ cup
- Eggs   2
- Italian breadcrumbs   ½ cup
- Parmesan cheese, grated freshly   ¼ cup
- Italian seasoning   1 teaspoon

- Dried basil   ½ teaspoon
- Onion powder   ½ teaspoon
- Garlic powder   ½ teaspoon
- Ground black pepper   ½ teaspoon
- Salt   1 teaspoon

Instructions:

1. Cut the eggplant into ½-inch rounds and then cut each round into ¼-inch sticks.
2. With paper towels, pat dry the eggplant sticks.
3. In a shallow bowl, place the flour.
4. In a second shallow bowl, crack the eggs and beat lightly.
5. In a third shallow bowl, mix the breadcrumbs, Parmesan cheese, Italian seasoning, basil, onion powder, garlic powder, salt, and black pepper.
6. Dredge the eggplant sticks in flour, then dip into beaten eggs, and finally coat with Parmesan mixture.
7. Arrange the coated eggplant sticks onto a platter and set them aside for about 5 minutes.
9. Meanwhile, switch on the air fryer, insert the fryer basket, grease it with olive oil, then set the cooking temperature to 370 degrees F (188 °C), and set frying time for 5 minutes or more to preheat the fryer.
8. After preheating, arrange the eggplant sticks into the greased air fryer basket.
9. Slide the basket into the air fryer and set the time for 15 minutes.
10. Shake the basket after 10 minutes of cooking.
11. When cooking time is completed, remove the eggplant sticks and serve warm.

Tip:

Don't forget to pat dry the eggplant slices before coating.

Air fryer Stuffed Bell Peppers

Prep Time:	15 minutes	Calories:	410
Cook Time:	15 minutes	Fat (g):	20.5
Total Time:	30 minutes	Protein (g):	29.5
Servings:	3	Carbs (g):	25.9

Ingredients:

- Red bell peppers, medium   3
- Olive oil   1 tablespoon
- Ground turkey   12 oz (340g)
- Cooked brown rice   ½ cup
- Panko breadcrumbs   ¼ cup
- Parmesan cheese, grated   ¼ cup
- Corn   ¼ cup

- Marinara sauce, low-sodium — ¾ cup
- Fresh parsley, chopped — 3 tablespoons
- Ground black pepper — ¼ teaspoon
- Mozzarella cheese, shredded — ¼ cup

Instructions:

1. Carefully cut the top of each bell pepper and reserve them.
2. Remove the seeds of each bell pepper.
3. In a large skillet, heat oil over medium-high heat and cook the turkey for about 4 minutes, stirring occasionally.
4. Stir in rice and breadcrumbs and cook for about 1 minute, stirring occasionally.
5. Remove from the heat and stir in the Parmesan cheese, corn, marinara sauce, parsley, and black pepper.
6. Divide the turkey mixture evenly among the bell peppers.
7. Switch on the air fryer, insert the fryer basket, grease it with olive oil, then set the cooking temperature to 350 degrees F (177 °C), and set frying time for 5 minutes or more to preheat the fryer.
8. After preheating, arrange the bell peppers into the greased air fryer basket.
9. Slide the basket into the air fryer and set the time for 10 minutes.
10. After 8 minutes of cooking, sprinkle each bell pepper with mozzarella cheese.
11. When cooking time is completed, remove the bell peppers and serve.

Tip:

You can use ground beef or pork instead of turkey.

Air fryer Fish Sticks

Prep Time:	10 minutes	Calories:	209
Cook Time:	12 minutes	Fat (g):	3
Total Time:	22 minutes	Protein (g):	18
Servings:	4	Carbs (g):	15

Ingredients:

- Cod fillets, skinless, cut into 1-inch strips   1 lb (453g)
- All-purpose flour   ½ cup
- Egg, beaten   1
- Panko breadcrumbs   ½ cup
- Lemon-pepper seasoning   ½ teaspoon
- Salt   ½ teaspoon
- Paprika   ½ teaspoon
- Cooking spray

Instructions:

1. In a shallow dish, place the flour.
2. In a second shallow dish, crack the eggs and beat lightly.
3. In a third shallow dish, mix the breadcrumbs, lemon-pepper seasoning, salt, and paprika.
4. Coat the cod sticks with flour, then dip into beaten egg and finally coat with breadcrumbs mixture.
5. Switch on the air fryer, insert the fryer basket, grease it with olive oil, then set the cooking temperature to 400 degrees F (204 °C), and set frying time for 5 minutes or more to preheat the fryer.
6. After preheating, arrange the cod sticks into the greased air fryer basket and spray with the cooking spray.
7. Slide the basket into the air fryer and set the time for 10-12 minutes.
8. After 5 minutes of cooking, flip the cod sticks and spray with the cooking spray.
9. When cooking time is completed, remove the cod sticks and serve.

Tip:

You can also use ½ teaspoon of Old Bay Seasoning.

Air fryer Calzones

Prep Time:	15 minutes	Calories:	157
Cook Time:	22 minutes	Fat (g):	4.6
Total Time:	37 minutes	Protein (g):	6
Servings:	9	Carbs (g):	21.3

Ingredients:

- Refrigerated pizza dough   1 (13.8-ounce) package
- Pizza sauce   9 teaspoons
- Pepperoni   1 (1¾-ounce) package
- Mozzarella cheese, shredded   4 ½ tablespoons
- Cooking spray

Instructions:

1. Place the pizza dough onto a lightly floured surface and roll it.
2. With a 2 1/8-inch biscuit cutter, cut the rolled dough into 9 equal-sized circles.
3. Then roll each dough circle into a 4½-inch disc.
4. Spread pizza sauce over each disc, followed by 3 pepperoni slices and mozzarella cheese.
5. Fold over and secure edges by pressing.
6. With the tines of a fork, crimp the edges.
7. Switch on the air fryer, insert the fryer basket, grease it with olive oil, then set the cooking temperature to 375 degrees F (190 °C), and set frying time for 5 minutes or more to preheat the fryer.
8. After preheating, line the air fryer basket with a greased parchment paper.
9. Arrange the calzones into the prepared air fryer basket in 2 batches and spray with the cooking spray.
10. Slide the basket into the air fryer and set the time for 9-11 minutes.
11. After 7 minutes of cooking, flip the calzones and spray with the cooking spray.
12. When cooking time is completed, remove the calzones and serve warm.

Tip:

Calzones are done when the crust is golden brown and sounds hollow when tapped.

Air fryer Spicy Green Beans

Prep Time:	10 minutes	Calories:	61
Cook Time:	24 minutes	Fat (g):	3.6
Total Time:	34 minutes	Protein (g):	1.8
Servings:	4	Carbs (g):	6.8

Ingredients:

- Garlic clove, minced   1
- Soy sauce   1 teaspoon
- Sesame oil   1 tablespoon
- Rice wine vinegar   1 teaspoon
- Red pepper flakes   ½ teaspoon
- Fresh green beans, trimmed   12 oz (340g)

Instructions:

1. In a bowl, add all ingredients except for green beans and beat until well combined.
2. Add the green beans and toss to coat well.
3. Set aside for about 5 minutes.
4. Switch on the air fryer, insert the fryer basket, grease it with olive oil, then set the cooking temperature to 400 degrees F (204 °C), and set frying time for 5 minutes or more to preheat the fryer.
5. After preheating, arrange the green beans into the greased air fryer basket in 2 batches.
6. Slide the basket into the air fryer and set the time for 12 minutes.
7. When cooking time is completed, remove the green beans and serve.

Tip:

You can garnish the green beans with Parmesan cheese.

Air fryer Banana Cake

Prep Time:	10 minutes	Calories:	352
Cook Time:	30 minutes	Fat (g):	11.7
Total Time:	40 minutes	Protein (g):	5.1
Servings:	4	Carbs (g):	57.9

Ingredients:

- Self-rising flour   1 cup
- Ground cinnamon   ½ teaspoon
- Pinch of salt
- Brown sugar   1/3 cup
- Butter, softened   3 ½ tablespoons
- Banana, peeled, and mashed   1

- Egg   1
- Honey   2 tablespoons

Instructions:

1. In a bowl, mix flour, cinnamon, and salt.
2. In another bowl, add the brown sugar and butter, and with an electric mixer, beat until creamy.
3. Add the banana, egg, and honey and beat until smooth.
4. Add the flour mixture and beat until smooth.
5. Place the mixture into a greased small fluted tube pan.
6. With a spatula, smooth the top surface.
7. Set the temperature of the air fryer to 320 degrees F (160 °C) to preheat.
8. After preheating, arrange the cake pan into the air fryer basket.
9. Slide the basket into the air fryer and set the time for 30 minutes.
10. When cooking time is completed, remove the cake pan and place it onto a wire rack for about 10 minutes.
11. Carefully invert the cake onto the wire rack to cool completely before serving.
12. Cut into desired-sized slices and serve.

Air fryer Buffalo Cauliflower Bites

Prep Time:	10 minutes	Calories:	209
Cook Time:	30 minutes	Fat (g):	17
Total Time:	40 minutes	Protein (g):	6
Servings:	4	Carbs (g):	14

Ingredients:

- Head cauliflower, cut into florets   1
- Butter, melted   2 tablespoons
- Hot sauce   ½ cup
- Olive oil   1 tablespoon
- Almond flour   ½ cup

- Dried parsley   3 tablespoons
- Salt   1 teaspoon
- Garlic powder   ½ tablespoon

Instructions:

1. In a bowl, add hot sauce, butter, and oil and mix well.
2. Add the cauliflower florets and toss to coat well.
3. In another bowl, mix the flour, parsley, salt, and garlic powder.
4. Add the cauliflower florets and toss to coat well.
5. Meanwhile, switch on the air fryer, insert the fryer basket, grease it with olive oil, then set the cooking temperature to 350 degrees F (177 °C), and set frying time for 5 minutes or more to preheat the fryer.
6. After preheating, arrange the cauliflower florets into the greased air fryer basket in 2 batches.
7. Slide the basket into the air fryer and set the time for 15 minutes.
8. While cooking, shake the air fryer basket twice.
9. When cooking time is completed, remove the cauliflower florets and serve.

Tip:

For more crunch, broil the cauliflower bites for 2 minutes after cooking in the air fryer.

Air fryer Kale Chips

Prep Time:	10 minutes	Calories:	58
Cook Time:	16 minutes	Fat (g):	5
Total Time:	26 minutes	Protein (g):	1
Servings:	6	Carbs (g):	2.3

Ingredients:

- Fresh kale leaves, stems removed, chopped   6 cups
- Olive oil   2 tablespoons
- Garlic powder   1 teaspoon
- Onion powder   ¼ teaspoon
- Salt   ½ teaspoon
- Ground black pepper   1/8 teaspoon

Instructions:

1. Switch on the air fryer, insert the fryer basket, grease it with olive oil, then set the cooking temperature to 360 degrees F (182 °C) and set frying time for 5 minutes or more to preheat the fryer.
2. In a bowl, place the kale and oil, and mix well with your hands.
3. Add the spices and toss to coat well.
4. After preheating, arrange the kale pieces into the greased air fryer basket in 2 batches.
5. Slide the basket into the air fryer and set the time for 8 minutes.
6. Shake the basket after 6 minutes of cooking.
7. When cooking time is completed, remove the kale chips and serve.

Tip:

You can also use curry powder for more flavoring.

Air fryer Beignets

Prep Time:	20 minutes	Calories:	207
Cook Time:	26 minutes	Fat (g):	7
Total Time:	46 minutes	Protein (g):	4.9
Servings:	9	Carbs (g):	31

Ingredients:

- Plain Greek yogurt   1 cup
- Granulated sugar   2 tablespoons
- Vanilla extract   1 teaspoon
- Self-rising flour   1 cup
- Unsalted butter, melted   2 tablespoons
- Powdered sugar   ½ cup

Instructions:

1. In a bowl, add the yogurt, granulated sugar, and vanilla extract and mix until well combined.
2. Add the flour and stir until dough forms.
3. Place the dough onto a floured surface.
4. Fold the dough over 2-3 times until smooth.
5. With your hands, pat the dough into a 4x5-inch (1-inch thick) rectangle.
6. Now cut the dough into 9 equal-sized pieces.
7. Dust both sides of the dough pieces with flour lightly.
8. Set aside for about 15 minutes.
9. Set the temperature of the air fryer to 350 degrees F (177 °C) to preheat.
10. Brush one side of beignets with melted butter.
11. After preheating, arrange the beignets, butter-side down into the greased air fryer basket in 2 batches.
12. Now brush the top of beignets with melted butter.
13. Slide the basket into the air fryer and set the time for 13 minutes.
14. After 7 minutes of cooking, flip the beignets.
15. When cooking time is completed, remove the beignets and place them onto a paper towel-lined plate.
16. Dust the beignets with powdered sugar generously and serve warm.

Tip:

Don't use flavored yogurt in this recipe.

Air fryer Apple Fritters

Prep Time:	15 minutes	Calories:	223
Cook Time:	30 minutes	Fat (g):	3
Total Time:	45 minutes	Protein (g):	3
Servings:	14	Carbs (g):	47

Ingredients:

<u>For Fritters:</u>

- Large apples, peeled, cored, and cut into ¼-inch pieces — 2
- All-purpose flour — 2 cups
- Granulated sugar — ½ cup
- Baking powder — 1 tablespoon
- Ground cinnamon — 1 teaspoon
- Ground nutmeg — ½ teaspoon
- Ground cloves — ¼ teaspoon
- Salt — 1 teaspoon

• Eggs	2
• Apple cider	¾ cup
• Butter, melted	3 tablespoons
• Vanilla extract	1 teaspoon
• Cooking spray	

For Glaze:

• Powdered sugar	2 cups
• Apple cider	¼ cup
• Ground cinnamon	½ teaspoon
• Ground nutmeg	¼ teaspoon

Instructions:

1. Spread the apple pieces onto a kitchen towel and pat dry them completely.
2. In a bowl, mix the flour, sugar, baking powder, spices, and salt.
3. Add the apple pieces and stir to combine.
4. In another bowl, add the eggs, apple cider, butter, vanilla extract, and beat until well combined.
5. Add the egg mixture into the flour mixture and mix until well combined.
6. Switch on the air fryer, insert the fryer basket, grease it with olive oil, then set the cooking temperature to 390 degrees F (199 °C), and set frying time for 5 minutes or more to preheat the fryer.
7. After preheating, with an ice cream scooper, place the fritters into the parchment paper-lined air fryer basket in 3 batches and spray the tops with cooking spray.
8. Slide the basket into the air fryer and set the time for 10 minutes.
9. After 6 minutes of cooking, flip the fritters and spray the tops with cooking spray.
10. Meanwhile, for glaze: in a bowl, add all ingredients and beat until smooth.
11. Set aside for about 10 minutes or until the glaze sets.
12. When cooking time is completed, remove the fritters and transfer them onto serving plates.
13. Drizzle with glaze and serve warm.

Tip:

Apple cider can be replaced with apple juice too.

Air fryer Chicken Tenders

Prep Time:	15 minutes	Calories:	298
Cook Time:	15 minutes	Fat (g):	7.5
Total Time:	30 minutes	Protein (g):	34
Servings:	4	Carbs (g):	23

Ingredients:

- All-purpose flour ½ cup
- Eggs, large 3
- Panko breadcrumbs ½ cup
- Garlic powder ½ teaspoon
- Salt and pepper To taste
- Chicken tenders 1 lb (453g)

Instructions:

1. In a shallow dish, place the flour.
2. In a second shallow dish, crack the eggs and beat lightly.
3. In a third shallow dish, mix the breadcrumbs, garlic powder, salt, and black pepper.
4. Coat the chicken tenders with flour, then dip into beaten egg and finally coat with breadcrumbs mixture.
5. Switch on the air fryer, insert the fryer basket, grease it with olive oil, then set the cooking temperature to 400 degrees F (204 °C), and set frying time for 5 minutes or more to preheat the fryer.
6. After preheating, arrange the chicken tenders into the greased air fryer basket and spray with cooking spray lightly.
7. Slide the basket into the air fryer and set the time for 15 minutes.
8. After 8 minutes of cooking, flip the chicken tenders and spray with cooking spray lightly.
9. When cooking time is completed, remove the chicken tenders and serve hot.

Air fryer Cannoli

Prep Time:	20 minutes	Calories:	239
Cook Time:	14 minutes	Fat (g):	15
Total Time:	34 minutes	Protein (g):	5
Servings:	16	Carbs (g):	18

Ingredients:

- Whole-milk ricotta cheese   1 (24-ounce) package
- Powdered sugar   ½ cup, plus more for dusting
- Orange zest, grated   1 tablespoon
- Salt   ½ teaspoon
- Brown sugar   1 cup
- Refrigerated piecrusts   1 (14.1-ounce) package
- Large egg white, beaten   1

- Mini chocolate chips   ½ cup
- Roasted pistachios, chopped   ½ cup

Instructions:

1. Line a strainer with a cheesecloth.
2. Place the ricotta cheese in the strainer and press to remove any excess liquid.
3. In a bowl, add the strained ricotta, powdered sugar, orange zest, and salt and mix well.
4. Place the ricotta mixture into a piping bag and refrigerate until ready to use.
5. In a shallow dish, place the brown sugar. Set aside.
6. Place the piecrusts onto a lightly floured surface and roll each into 1/16-inch thickness.
7. Cut 16 (3½-inch) circles from piecrusts.
8. Wrap circles around cannoli molds and brush the edges with egg white to seal.
9. Now brush the wrapper with egg white lightly.
10. Coat each wrapper with brown sugar evenly.
11. Switch on the air fryer, insert the fryer basket, grease it with olive oil, then set the cooking temperature to 400 degrees F (204 °C), and set frying time for 5 minutes or more to preheat the fryer.
12. After preheating, arrange the wrappers into the greased air fryer basket in 2 batches.
13. Slide the basket into the air fryer and set the time for 7 minutes.
14. When cooking time is completed, remove the wrappers and place them onto a platter.
15. Set aside to cool for about 1 minute.
16. Gently twist cannoli mold out of the shell and set aside to cool completely.
17. In 2 shallow bowls, place chocolate chips and pistachios.
18. Pipe ricotta mixture into each cooled cannoli shell.
19. Dip one end into chocolate chips, then dip into the pistachios.
20. Dust with powdered sugar and serve immediately.

Tip:

Make sure to strain the ricotta before using it.

Air fryer Chicken Taquitos

Prep Time:	25 minutes	Calories:	178
Cook Time:	15 minutes	Fat (g):	8
Total Time:	40 minutes	Protein (g):	14.8
Servings:	12	Carbs (g):	12.1

Ingredients:

- Cooked chicken, shredded — 3 cups
- Salsa — ½ cup
- Monterey Jack cheese, shredded — 1 cup
- Cream cheese, softened — 4 oz (113g)
- Red chili powder — 1 teaspoon
- Ground cumin — 1 teaspoon
- Garlic powder — 1 teaspoon

- Small flour tortillas   12
- Salt and pepper   To taste
- Cooking spray

Instructions:

1. In a bowl, add all ingredients except for tortillas and mix until well combined.
2. Arrange the tortillas onto a smooth surface.
3. Place the chicken mixture over each tortilla and then roll them tightly.
4. Spray the taquitos.
5. Switch on the air fryer, insert the fryer basket, grease it with olive oil, then set the cooking temperature to 400 degrees F (204 °C), and set frying time for 5 minutes or more to preheat the fryer.
6. After preheating, arrange the taquitos into the greased air fryer basket.
7. Slide the basket into the air fryer and set the time for 12-15 minutes.
8. When cooking time is completed, remove the taquitos and serve warm.

Tip:

You can secure the rolls with toothpicks.

Air fryer Cheeseburger

Prep Time:	15 minutes	Calories:	515
Cook Time:	14 minutes	Fat (g):	14.9
Total Time:	29 minutes	Protein (g):	45.2
Servings:	4	Carbs (g):	40.3

Ingredients:

- Ground beef   1 lb (453g)
- Worcestershire sauce   1 teaspoon
- Weber Burger Seasoning   1 ½ tablespoons
- Salt and pepper   To taste
- Cheddar cheese slices   4
- Buns   4

- Lettuce leaves   8
- Tomato, cut into slices   1

Instructions:

1. For patties: in a bowl, add the ground beef, Worcestershire sauce, burger seasoning, salt, and black pepper, and mix until well combined.
2. Make 4 patties from the mixture.
3. Switch on the air fryer, insert the fryer basket, grease it with olive oil, then set the cooking temperature to 360 degrees F (182 °C) and set frying time for 5 minutes or more to preheat the fryer.
4. After preheating, arrange the patties into the greased air fryer basket.
5. Slide the basket into the air fryer and set the time for 14 minutes.
6. Flip the burgers after 6 minutes of cooking.
7. After 12 minutes, place 1 cheese slice over each patty.
8. When cooking time is completed, remove the patties and serve over buns with lettuce and tomatoes.

Tip:

You can use seasoning of your choice.

Air fryer Chicken Breast

Prep Time:	10 minutes	Calories:	165
Cook Time:	22 minutes	Fat (g):	3
Total Time:	32 minutes	Protein (g):	30
Servings:	4	Carbs (g):	0

Ingredients:

- Chicken breasts, boneless, skinless   4
- Salt   ½ teaspoon
- Ground black pepper   1/8 teaspoon
- Garlic powder   ½ teaspoon
- Dried oregano   ½ teaspoon

- Cooking spray

Instructions:

1. In a small bowl, mix the oregano and spices.
2. Spray the chicken breasts with cooking spray and sprinkle with a spice mixture.
3. Switch on the air fryer, insert the fryer basket, grease it with olive oil, then set the cooking temperature to 360 degrees F (182 °C) and set frying time for 5 minutes or more to preheat the fryer.
4. After preheating, arrange the chicken breasts into the greased air fryer basket.
5. Slide the basket into the air fryer and set the time for 20-22 minutes.
6. After 10 minutes of cooking, flip the chicken breasts.
7. When cooking time is completed, remove the chicken breasts and serve hot.

Air fryer Buttermilk Fried Chicken

Prep Time:	15 minutes	Calories:	321
Cook Time:	25 minutes	Fat (g):	15
Total Time:	40 minutes	Protein (g):	21
Servings:	4	Carbs (g):	22

Ingredients:

For Marinade:
- Buttermilk   ½ cup
- Hot sauce   ½ cup
- Whole chicken cut into separate pieces   ½
  (breast, thigh, wing, and leg)

For Seasoning:
- All-purpose flour   ¾ cup

- Italian seasoning   1 teaspoon
- Seasoning salt   2 teaspoons
- Onion powder   1 teaspoon
- Garlic powder   1 teaspoon
- Cayenne pepper   ½ teaspoon
- Cooking spray

Instructions:

1. In a large bowl, mix the buttermilk and hot sauce.
2. Add the chicken pieces and marinate for about 1 hour in the refrigerator.
3. For seasoning: in a shallow bowl, add all ingredients and mix well.
4. After 1 hour, remove the chicken pieces from the buttermilk mixture and coat them evenly with flour mixture.
5. Then shake off any excess flour.
6. Switch on the air fryer, insert the fryer basket, grease it with olive oil, then set the cooking temperature to 400 degrees F (204 °C), and set frying time for 5 minutes or more to preheat the fryer.
7. After preheating, arrange the chicken pieces into the parchment paper-lined air fryer basket.
8. Slide the basket into the air fryer and set the time for 25 minutes.
9. After 13 minutes of cooking, spray the chicken pieces with cooking spray.
10. Flip the chicken pieces and spray again.
11. When cooking time is completed, remove the chicken pieces and serve hot.

Tip:

Adjust the seasoning according to your taste.

Air fryer Cinnamon Rolls

Prep Time:	15 minutes	Calories:	255
Cook Time:	7 minutes	Fat (g):	16
Total Time:	22 minutes	Protein (g):	2
Servings:	8	Carbs (g):	25

Ingredients:

For Cinnamon rolls:
- Unsalted butter, softened   ¼ cup
- Brown sugar   6 tablespoons
- Ground cinnamon   1 tablespoon
- Puff pastry sheet, thawed   1

<u>For Icing:</u>

• Powdered sugar	½ cup
• Milk	1 tablespoon
• Fresh lemon juice	2 teaspoons

Instructions:

1. In a small bowl, add the butter, sugar, and cinnamon and mix well.
2. Place the puff pastry onto a smooth surface and gently roll it.
3. Place the cinnamon mixture over the pastry in a thin layer.
4. Starting from the shorter end, roll the pastry gently and loosely.
5. With a serrated knife, cut the pastry into 1-inch pieces.
6. Switch on the air fryer, insert the fryer basket, grease it with olive oil, then set the cooking temperature to 400 degrees F (204 °C), and set frying time for 5 minutes or more to preheat the fryer.
7. After preheating, arrange the roll pieces into the greased air fryer basket.
8. Slide the basket into the air fryer and set the time for 7 minutes.
9. When cooking time is completed, remove the roll pieces and place them onto a platter to cool slightly before icing.
10. For the icing: in a bowl, add all the ingredients and beat until well combined.
11. Drizzle the rolls with icing and serve warm.

Tip:

Make sure to use chilled puff pastry.

Air fryer Sesame Chicken

Prep Time:	20 minutes	Calories:	345
Cook Time:	24 minutes	Fat (g):	12
Total Time:	44 minutes	Protein (g):	32
Servings:	6	Carbs (g):	28

Ingredients:

For chicken thighs:
- Chicken thighs, boneless, skinless, cubed   6
- Cornstarch   ½ cup
- Cooking spray

For sauce:
- Soy sauce   ¼ cup
- Fresh orange juice   2 tablespoons

- Hoisin sauce — 5 teaspoons
- Brown sugar — 2 tablespoons
- Ground ginger — ½ teaspoon
- Garlic clove, crushed — 1
- Cornstarch — 1 tablespoon
- Coldwater — 1 tablespoon
- Sesame seeds — 2 teaspoons

For serving:
- Cooked rice — Optional
- Scallion greens, chopped — Optional

Instructions:

1. In a bowl, add the chicken cubes and cornstarch and toss to coat well.
2. Switch on the air fryer, insert the fryer basket, grease it with olive oil, then set the cooking temperature to 390 degrees F (199 °C) and set frying time for 5 minutes or more to preheat the fryer.
3. After preheating, arrange the chicken cubes into the greased air fryer basket and spray with cooking spray.
4. Slide the basket into the air fryer and set the time for 24 minutes.
5. Flip the chicken cubes once halfway through and spray with cooking spray.
6. Meanwhile, for the sauce: in a small saucepan, add all ingredients except for cornstarch and water and mix until well combined.
7. Place the saucepan over medium-high heat and bring to a gentle simmer, stirring continuously.
8. Meanwhile, in a small bowl, dissolve the cornstarch in water.
9. Add the cornstarch mixture into the pan, stirring continuously.
10. Cook for about 5 minutes.
11. Remove the sauce from the heat and set aside for 5 minutes to thicken.
12. When cooking time is completed, remove the chicken cubes from the air fryer basket and transfer them into a bowl.
13. Add the sauce and toss to coat well.
14. Serve the chicken with rice and scallion greens.

Air fryer Shrimp Fajitas

Prep Time:	15 minutes	Calories:	111
Cook Time:	22 minutes	Fat (g):	1.4
Total Time:	37 minutes	Protein (g):	10
Servings:	12	Carbs (g):	14

Ingredients:

- Medium shrimp, peeled and deveined   1 lb (453g)
- Green bell pepper, seeded and chopped   1
- Red bell pepper, seeded and chopped   1
- Sweet onion, chopped   ½ cup
- Fajita seasoning   2 tablespoons
- Tortillas   12
- Cooking spray

Instructions:

1. In a bowl, add all ingredients and spray with cooking spray.
2. Then toss to coat well.
3. Switch on the air fryer, insert the fryer basket, grease it with olive oil, then set the cooking temperature to 390 degrees F (199 °C) and set frying time for 5 minutes or more to preheat the fryer.
4. After preheating, arrange the shrimp mixture into the greased air fryer basket.
5. Slide the basket into the air fryer and set the time for 22 minutes.
6. After 12 minutes of cooking, spray the shrimp mixture with cooking spray and stir to combine.
7. When cooking time is completed, remove the shrimp mixture and transfer it into a bowl.
8. Arrange the warm tortillas onto serving plates.
9. Top each tortilla with a shrimp mixture and serve.

Tip:

Taco seasoning can also be used instead of Fajita seasoning.

Air fryer Baked Apples

Prep Time:	10 minutes	Calories:	161
Cook Time:	20 minutes	Fat (g):	7.8
Total Time:	30 minutes	Protein (g):	2.5
Servings:	2	Carbs (g):	23.7

Ingredients:

- Apple, medium — 1
- Raisins — 2 tablespoons
- Walnuts, chopped — 2 tablespoons
- Butter, melted — 1 ½ teaspoons
- Ground nutmeg — ¼ teaspoon
- Water — ¼ cup
- Ground cinnamon — ¼ teaspoon

Instructions:

1. In a bowl, mix the raisins, walnuts, butter, cinnamon, and nutmeg.
2. Cut the apple in half around the middle, and with a scooper, scoop out some flesh.
3. Stuff each apple half with a raisin mixture.
4. Arrange the baking pan into the air fryer basket.
5. Set the temperature of the air fryer to 350 degrees F (177 °C) to preheat.
6. After preheating, arrange the apple halves into the baking pan.
7. Carefully place the water into the baking pan.
8. Set the time for 20 minutes.
9. When cooking time is completed, remove the apple halves and serve warm.

Tip:

Pear can also be used in this recipe instead of apple.

Air fryer Sweet Potato Fries

Prep Time:	10 minutes	Calories:	239
Cook Time:	20 minutes	Fat (g):	5
Total Time:	30 minutes	Protein (g):	4
Servings:	2	Carbs (g):	46

Ingredients:

- Sweet potato, unpeeled and cut into ¼-½-inch thick slices — 16 oz (453g)
- Avocado oil — 2 teaspoons
- Sea salt — ½ teaspoon
- Ground black pepper — ¼ teaspoon
- Paprika — ¼ teaspoon

Instructions:

1. In a bowl, add all ingredients and toss to coat well.
2. Switch on the air fryer, insert the fryer basket, grease it with olive oil, then set the cooking temperature to 390 degrees F (199 °C) and set frying time for 5 minutes or more to preheat the fryer.
3. After preheating, arrange the sweet potato slices into the greased air fryer basket.
4. Slide the basket into the air fryer and set the time for 20 minutes.
5. While cooking, shake the air fryer basket occasionally.
6. When cooking time is completed, remove the sweet potato fries and serve warm.

Air fryer Fried Rice

Prep Time:	10 minutes	Calories:	248
Cook Time:	15 minutes	Fat (g):	6.1
Total Time:	25 minutes	Protein (g):	6.9
Servings:	4	Carbs (g):	39.7

Ingredients:

- Cooked rice   3 cups
- Frozen vegetables (carrot, corn, broccoli)   1 cup
- Scrambled eggs   2
- Coconut aminos   1/3 cup
- Olive oil   1 tablespoon

Instructions:

1. In a bowl, add all ingredients and stir to combine.
2. Place the mixture into a baking pan.
3. Switch on the air fryer, insert the fryer basket, then set cooking temperature to 360 degrees F (182 °C) and set frying time for 5 minutes or more to preheat the fryer.
4. After preheating, arrange the baking pan into the air fryer basket.
5. Slide the basket into the air fryer and set the time for 15 minutes.
6. While cooking, stir the rice mixture every 4 minutes.
7. When cooking time is completed, remove the baking pan and serve.

Tip:

You can use any combinations of frozen veggies of your choice.

Air fryer Grill Cheese

Prep Time:	10 minutes	Calories:	340
Cook Time:	3 minutes	Fat (g):	22.4
Total Time:	13 minutes	Protein (g):	9
Servings:	2	Carbs (g):	26

Ingredients:

- Sourdough bread slices 4
- Butter, softened .... 2 tablespoons
- Sharp cheddar cheese slices 2
- Havarti cheese slices 2

Instructions:

1. Switch on the air fryer, insert the fryer basket, grease it with olive oil, then set the cooking temperature to 375 degrees F (190 °C), and set frying time for 5 minutes or more to preheat the fryer.
2. Spread the butter on 1 side of each bread slice evenly.
3. After preheating, arrange 2 bread slices into the greased air fryer basket, buttered-side down.
4. Arrange 1 Cheddar cheese slice and 1 Havarti cheese slice over each bread slice.
5. Top with remaining bread slices, buttered side up.
6. Slide the basket into the air fryer and set the time for 3 minutes.
7. When cooking time is completed, remove the sandwiches and place them onto a platter.
8. Cut each sandwich in half and serve.

Tip:

You can use Monterrey Jack cheese instead of Havarti cheese.

Air fryer Spicy Dill Pickle Fries

Prep Time:	15 minutes	Calories:	77
Cook Time:	28 minutes	Fat (g):	0.8
Total Time:	43 minutes	Protein (g):	3.2
Servings:	12	Carbs (g):	17

Ingredients:

- All-purpose flour   1 cup
- Paprika   ½ teaspoon
- Egg   1
- Milk   ¼ cup
- Panko breadcrumbs   1 cup
- Spicy dill pickle spears, drained and pat   1½ (16-ounce) jars
  dried
- Cooking spray

Instructions:

1. In a shallow dish, mix the flour and paprika.
2. In a second shallow bowl, add the egg and milk and beat lightly.
3. In a third shallow bowl, place the breadcrumbs.
4. Coat the pickle spears with the flour mixture, then dip into the egg mixture and finally coat with breadcrumbs.
5. Spray the pickle spears with cooking spray lightly.
6. Switch on the air fryer, insert the fryer basket, grease it with olive oil, then set the cooking temperature to 400 degrees F (204 °C), and set frying time for 5 minutes or more to preheat the fryer.
7. After preheating, arrange the pickle spears into the greased air fryer basket in 2 batches.
8. Slide the basket into the air fryer and set the time for 14 minutes.
9. Flip the pickle spears once halfway through.
10. When cooking time is completed, remove the pickle fries and serve.

Tip:

Serve with your favorite dipping sauce.

Air fryer Mushrooms

Prep Time:	10 minutes	Calories:	169
Cook Time:	10 minutes	Fat (g):	13.4
Total Time:	20 minutes	Protein (g):	6.7
Servings:	2	Carbs (g):	4.5

Ingredients:

- Cremini mushrooms, sliced   1 (8-ounce) package
- Avocado oil   2 tablespoons
- Soy sauce   1 teaspoon
- Salt and pepper   To taste
- Garlic powder   ½ teaspoon

Instructions:

1. Switch on the air fryer, insert the fryer basket, grease it with olive oil, then set the cooking temperature to 375 degrees F (190 °C), and set frying time for 5 minutes or more to preheat the fryer.
2. In a bowl, add all ingredients and toss to coat well.
3. After preheating, arrange the mushrooms into the greased air fryer basket.
4. Slide the basket into the air fryer and set the time for 10 minutes.
5. While cooking, shake the air fryer basket occasionally.
6. When cooking time is completed, remove the mushrooms and serve.

Air fryer Pork Tenderloin

Prep Time:	10 minutes	Calories:	273
Cook Time:	22 minutes	Fat (g):	8.9
Total Time:	32 minutes	Protein (g):	44.2
Servings:	4	Carbs (g):	3.3

Ingredients:

- Brown sugar   2 tablespoons
- Ground mustard   1 teaspoon
- Smoked paprika   1 tablespoon
- Onion powder   ½ teaspoon
- Garlic powder   ¼ teaspoon
- Cayenne powder   ¼ teaspoon
- Salt   1 ½ teaspoons

- Ground black pepper   ½ teaspoon
- Pork tenderloin, trimmed   1½ lbs (680g)
- Olive oil   ½ tablespoon

Instructions:

1. In a bowl, mix the brown sugar, mustard, and spices.
2. Coat the pork tenderloin with oil and then rub with spice mixture generously.
3. Switch on the air fryer, insert the fryer basket, grease it with olive oil, then set the cooking temperature to 400 degrees F (204 °C), and set frying time for 5 minutes or more to preheat the fryer.
4. After preheating, arrange the pork tenderloin into the greased air fryer basket.
5. Slide the basket into the air fryer and set the time for 20-22 minutes.
6. When cooking time is completed, remove the pork tenderloin and place it onto a cutting board for about 5 minutes before slicing.
7. Cut into desired-sized slices and serve.

Tip:

Don't forget to remove the silver skin from the pork tenderloin.

Air fryer Chocolate Chip Cookies

Prep Time:	15 minutes	Calories:	271
Cook Time:	12 minutes	Fat (g):	15
Total Time:	27 minutes	Protein (g):	3
Servings:	6	Carbs (g):	34

Ingredients:

- All-purpose flour   2/3 cup
- Baking soda   ¼ teaspoon
- Salt   1/8 teaspoon
- Unsalted butter, softened   ¼ cup
- Brown sugar   1/3 cup
- White sugar   2 tablespoons
- Egg yolk   1

- Vanilla extract   ½ teaspoon
- Semi-sweet chocolate chips   ½ cup

Instructions:

1. In a bowl, mix the flour, baking soda, and salt.
2. In another bowl, add the butter and sugars and beat until creamy.
3. Add the egg yolk and vanilla extract and beat until well combined.
4. Add the flour mixture and mix until the dough is just combined.
5. Add the chocolate chips and gently stir to combine.
6. Switch on the air fryer, insert the fryer basket, then set cooking temperature to 350 degrees F (177 °C) and set frying time for 5 minutes or more to preheat the fryer.
7. After preheating, with a spoon, place the dough into the foil-lined air fryer basket in 2 batches.
8. Slide the basket into the air fryer and set the time for 6 minutes.
9. When cooking time is completed, remove the cookies and place them onto a wire rack to cool completely before serving.

Tip:

For extra crunch, add chopped nuts like walnuts or pecans to the dough.

Air fryer Turkey Breast

Prep Time:	10 minutes	Calories:	231
Cook Time:	60 minutes	Fat (g):	10
Total Time:	1 h 10 m	Protein (g):	32.5
Servings:	10	Carbs (g):	0

Ingredients:

- Turkey breast, bone-in, skin-on   4 lbs (1814g)
- Olive oil   1 tablespoon
- Salt   2 teaspoons
- Poultry seasoning   ½ tablespoon

Instructions:

1. Coat the turkey breast with oil and then rub with salt and poultry seasoning.
2. Switch on the air fryer, insert the fryer basket, grease it with olive oil, then set the cooking temperature to 350 degrees F (177 °C) and set frying time for 5 minutes or more to preheat the fryer.
3. After preheating, arrange the turkey breast into the greased air fryer basket, skin side down.
4. Slide the basket into the air fryer and set the time for 50-60 minutes.
5. After 20 minutes of cooking, flip the turkey breast.
6. When cooking time is completed, remove the turkey breast and place it onto a cutting board for about 10 minutes before slicing.
7. Cut into desired-sized slices and serve.

Air fryer Egg Rolls

Prep Time:	20 minutes	Calories:	142
Cook Time:	1 h 10 m	Fat (g):	7
Total Time:	1 h 30 m	Protein (g):	10
Servings:	20	Carbs (g):	9

Ingredients:

- Soy sauce   ¼ cup
- Sesame oil   1 teaspoon
- White granulated sugar   ½ teaspoon
- Chinese five-spice powder   ½ teaspoon
- Salt   ½ teaspoon
- Ground pork   1 ½ lbs (680g)
- Garlic cloves, minced   2
- Ginger, grated   2 teaspoons

- Cabbage, shredded   3 cups
- Carrot, peeled and shredded   1
- Scallions, chopped   4
- Egg roll wrappers   20
- Olive oil   3 tablespoons

Instructions:

1. In a bowl, add the soy sauce, sesame oil, sugar, five-spice powder, and salt and mix well. Set aside.
2. Heat a non-stick skillet over medium heat and cook the pork with garlic and ginger for about 4-5 minutes or until lightly brown.
3. Add the sauce and stir to combine.
4. Add the cabbage, carrots, and scallions and cook for about 5 minutes, stirring frequently.
5. Remove from the heat and set aside to cool slightly.
6. Arrange 1 roll wrapper onto a smooth surface.
7. With your wet finger, moisten the edges of the wrapper.
8. Place about 3 tablespoons of pork mixture in the center of the wrapper.
9. Fold the bottom corner up over the filling and bring the left and right corners to the center, pressing gently.
10. Roll the egg roll and place it seam side down on a lightly oiled non-stick baking sheet.
11. Repeat with remaining wrappers and filling.
12. Brush the rolls with oil evenly.
13. Switch on the air fryer, insert the fryer basket, grease it with olive oil, then set the cooking temperature to 400 degrees F (204 °C), and set frying time for 5 minutes or more to preheat the fryer.
14. After preheating, arrange the rolls, seam side down into the greased air fryer basket in 5 batches.
15. Slide the basket into the air fryer and set the time for 12 minutes.
16. Flip the rolls once halfway through.
17. When cooking time is completed, remove the rolls and serve warm.

Air fryer Chicken Schnitzel

Prep Time:	15 minutes	Calories:	449
Cook Time:	12 minutes	Fat (g):	20
Total Time:	27 minutes	Protein (g):	33
Servings:	4	Carbs (g):	33

Ingredients:

- Plain flour   14 oz (396g)
- Dried tarragon   1 tablespoon
- Salt and pepper   To taste
- Eggs, beaten   3
- Garlic puree   1 teaspoon
- Breadcrumbs   14 oz (396g)
- Mixed herbs   1 tablespoon
- Chicken breasts, large, butterflied   2

Instructions:

1. In a shallow dish, mix the flour, tarragon, salt, and black pepper.
2. In a second shallow bowl, add eggs, garlic puree, salt, and black pepper and mix well.
3. In a third shallow bowl, mix the breadcrumbs, mixed herbs, salt, and black pepper.
4. Coat the chicken breasts with flour mixture, then dip into the egg mixture and finally coat with breadcrumbs mixture.
5. Switch on the air fryer, insert the fryer basket, grease it with olive oil, then set the cooking temperature to 360 degrees F (182 °C) and set frying time for 5 minutes or more to preheat the fryer.
6. After preheating, arrange the chicken breasts into the greased air fryer basket.
7. Slide the basket into the air fryer and set the time for 12 minutes.
8. After 8 minutes of cooking, flip the chicken breasts.
9. Set the temperature to 400 degrees F (204 °C) and continue cooking for 4 minutes.
10. When cooking time is completed, remove the chicken breasts and place them onto a platter.
11. Cut each chicken breast in half and serve.

Air fryer Calamari

Prep Time:	15 minutes	Calories:	315
Cook Time:	24 minutes	Fat (g):	14
Total Time:	39 minutes	Protein (g):	25
Servings:	4	Carbs (g):	43

Ingredients:

- Buttermilk   1 cup
- Egg   1
- Squid rings   1 ¼ lbs (567g)
- Panko breadcrumbs   2 cups
- Salt   2 tablespoons
- Cracked pepper   2 tablespoons
- All-purpose flour   1 cup

Instructions:

1. In a shallow bowl, add egg and buttermilk and mix well.
2. In a second shallow dish, mix the breadcrumbs, flour, salt, and cracked pepper.
3. Dip the squid rings into the egg mixture and finally coat with bread-crumbs mixture.
4. Switch on the air fryer, insert the fryer basket, grease it with olive oil, then set the cooking temperature to 400 degrees F (204 °C), and set frying time for 5 minutes or more to preheat the fryer.
5. After preheating, arrange the squid rings into the greased air fryer basket in 2 batches.
6. Slide the basket into the air fryer and set the time for 10-12 minutes.
7. Flip the rings once halfway through.
8. When cooking time is completed, remove the squid rings and serve.

Tip:

You can adjust the level of seasoning to your taste preferences.

Air fryer Zucchini Corn Fritters

Prep Time:	25 minutes	Calories:	154
Cook Time:	12 minutes	Fat (g):	3.3
Total Time:	37 minutes	Protein (g):	6.8
Servings:	4	Carbs (g):	26.5

Ingredients:

- Medium zucchini, grated   2
- Medium cooked potato, mashed   1
- Corn kernels   1 cup
- Garlic cloves, minced   3
- Chickpea flour   2 tablespoons
- Olive oil   2 teaspoons
- Salt and pepper   To taste

For Sauce:

• Yogurt	½ cup
• Tahini	1 teaspoon
• Salt	To taste

Instructions:

1. In a bowl, place the grated zucchini and a little salt and mix well.
2. Set aside for about 10-15 minutes.
3. With your hands, squeeze the zucchini to remove any excess water.
4. In a bowl, add the zucchini and remaining ingredients except for oil and mix until well combined.
5. Make equal-sized patties from the mixture.
6. Brush each patty with oil evenly.
7. Switch on the air fryer, insert the fryer basket, grease it with olive oil, then set the cooking temperature to 360 degrees F (182 °C) and set frying time for 5 minutes or more to preheat the fryer.
8. After preheating, arrange the patties into the greased air fryer basket.
9. Slide the basket into the air fryer and set the time for 12 minutes.
10. After 8 minutes of cooking, flip the patties.
11. Meanwhile, for the sauce: in a bowl, add all ingredients and mix well.
12. When cooking time is completed, remove the patties and serve alongside yogurt sauce.

Tip:

You can also use all-purpose flour instead of chickpea flour.

Air fryer Jalapeño Poppers

Prep Time:	15 minutes	Calories:	204
Cook Time:	27 minutes	Fat (g):	17.4
Total Time:	42 minutes	Protein (g):	5.1
Servings:	4	Carbs (g):	7.6

Ingredients:

- Large jalapeño chiles — 8
- Cheddar cheese, shredded — 6 oz (170g)
- Cream cheese, softened — 4 oz (113g)
- Salt, divided — 1½ teaspoons
- All-purpose flour — ½ cup
- Large eggs — 2
- Panko breadcrumbs, crushed very finely — 1 ½ cups

- Sour cream   ½ cup
- Fresh lime juice   2 teaspoons
- Lime zest   ½ teaspoon

Instructions:

1. In a pan of boiling water, add the jalapeños over high heat and cook for about 3 minutes, stirring occasionally.
2. Drain the jalapeños and transfer them into a bowl of ice water for about 30 seconds.
3. With a knife, make a slit vertically along the side of each jalapeño.
4. Carefully remove the seeds.
5. Rinse the jalapeños and pat dry thoroughly.
6. In a bowl, add the Cheddar, cream cheese, and ½ teaspoon of salt and mix well.
7. Stuff each jalapeño with a cheese mixture.
8. In a shallow dish, place the flour.
9. In a second shallow dish, crack the eggs and beat lightly.
10. In a third shallow dish, mix the breadcrumbs and remaining salt.
11. Coat the jalapeños with flour, then dip into beaten eggs and finally coat with breadcrumbs mixture.
12. Spray the jalapeños with cooking spray.
13. Switch on the air fryer, insert the fryer basket, grease it with olive oil, then set the cooking temperature to 375 degrees F (190 °C), and set frying time for 5 minutes or more to preheat the fryer.
14. After preheating, arrange the jalapeños into the greased air fryer basket in 2 batches
15. Slide the basket into the air fryer and set the time for 10-12 minutes.
16. Flip the jalapeños once halfway through.
17. Meanwhile, in a bowl, add the sour cream, lime juice, and lime zest and mix well.
18. When cooking time is completed, remove the jalapeños and serve warm alongside the sour cream mixture.

Air fryer Lava Cake

Prep Time:	15 minutes	Calories:	529
Cook Time:	11 minutes	Fat (g):	41
Total Time:	26 minutes	Protein (g):	5
Servings:	3	Carbs (g):	37

Ingredients:

• Semi-sweet chocolate bar, chopped	4 oz (113g)
• Unsalted butter, cut into pieces	6 tablespoons
• Large egg	1
• Large egg yolk	1
• White sugar	3 tablespoons
• Vanilla extract	½ teaspoons
• All-purpose flour	3 tablespoons
• Pinch of salt	

Instructions:

1. Grease 3 6-ounce ramekins and set aside.
2. In a microwave-safe bowl, place chocolate and butter and microwave for about 1- 1 ½ minutes or until melted, stirring after every 30 seconds.
3. Remove from microwave and stir until smooth. Set aside.
4. In another large bowl, add egg, egg yolk, sugar, and vanilla extract, and with an electric beater, beat until well combined.
5. Add the chocolate mixture, flour, and salt and beat until combined.
6. Place the mixture into greased 3 (6-ounce) ramekins.
7. Set the temperature of the air fryer to 375 degrees F (190 °C) to preheat.
8. After preheating, arrange the ramekins into the air fryer basket.
9. Slide the basket into the air fryer and set the time for 10 minutes.
10. When cooking time is completed, remove the ramekins and set them aside to cool for about 1 minute.
11. Carefully invert the cakes from ramekins and serve.

Air fryer Banana Muffins

Prep Time:	10 minutes	Calories:	163
Cook Time:	15 minutes	Fat (g):	8
Total Time:	25 minutes	Protein (g):	2
Servings:	10	Carbs (g):	23

Ingredients:

• Ripe bananas, peeled	2
• Brown sugar	½ cup
• Olive oil	1/3 cup
• Egg	1
• Vanilla extract	1 teaspoon
• Self-rising flour	¾ cup
• Ground cinnamon	1 teaspoon

Instructions:

1. In a large bowl, place the bananas, and with a fork, mash them well.
2. Add the brown sugar, olive oil, egg, and vanilla extract and beat until well combined.
3. Add flour and cinnamon and mix until just combined.
4. Place the mixture into the silicone muffin holders.
5. Set the temperature of the air fryer to 320 degrees F (160 °C) to preheat.
6. After preheating, arrange the cupcake holders into the air fryer basket.
7. Slide the basket into the air fryer and set the time for 15 minutes.
8. When cooking time is completed, remove the cupcake holders and place them onto a wire rack to cool completely before serving.

Tip:

Make sure to use very ripe bananas; otherwise, you won't get that sweet banana flavor.

Air fryer Hot Dogs

Prep Time:	5 minutes	Calories:	233
Cook Time:	8 minutes	Fat (g):	8
Total Time:	13 minutes	Protein (g):	10
Servings:	6	Carbs (g):	30

Ingredients:

- Hot dogs   6
- Hot dog buns   6

Instructions:

1. Switch on the air fryer, insert the fryer basket, grease it with olive oil, then set the cooking temperature to 400 degrees F (204 °C), and set frying time for 5 minutes or more to preheat the fryer.
2. After preheating, arrange the hot dogs into the greased air fryer basket.
3. Slide the basket into the air fryer and set the time for 6 minutes.
4. When cooking time is completed, remove the hot dogs.
5. Arrange 1 hot dog in each bun and place it into the air fryer basket.
6. Slide the basket into the air fryer and set the time for 2 minutes.
7. When cooking time is completed, remove the hot dog buns and serve.

Tip:

Feel free to add sauces of your choice into the buns.

Air fryer Korean Fried Chicken

Prep Time:	15 minutes	Calories:	424
Cook Time:	25 minutes	Fat (g):	18.2
Total Time:	40 minutes	Protein (g):	44.1
Servings:	3	Carbs (g):	19.8

Ingredients:

For Chicken:
- Chicken wings   1 lb (453g)
- Olive oil   1 tablespoon
- Corn starch   3 tablespoons
- Salt and black pepper   To taste
- Cooking spray

For Sauce:
- Honey   1 tablespoon

• Ketchup	1 tablespoon
• Gochujang	1 tablespoon
• Brown sugar	1 tablespoon
• Sesame oil, toasted	½ tablespoon
• Soy sauce	½ tablespoon
• Garlic cloves, crushed	2
• Ginger, grated	½ tablespoon

Instructions:

1. Coat the chicken wings with oil and then season with salt and black pepper evenly.
2. In a bowl, place the wings and corn starch and toss to coat well.
3. Switch on the air fryer, insert the fryer basket, grease it with olive oil, then set the cooking temperature to 400 degrees F (204 °C), and set frying time for 5 minutes or more to preheat the fryer.
4. After preheating, arrange the chicken wings into the greased air fryer basket.
5. Slide the basket into the air fryer and set the time for 20 minutes.
6. Meanwhile, for the sauce: in a small saucepan, add all ingredients over medium heat and bring to a boil, stirring occasionally.
7. Remove from the heat and set aside.
8. After 15 minutes of cooking, flip the chicken wings.
9. When cooking time is completed, remove the chicken wings and place them onto a rack to cool for about 5 minutes.
10. Then spray the wings with cooking spray lightly.
11. Arrange the chicken wings into the greased air fryer basket.
12. Again set the temperature of the air fryer to 400 degrees F (204 °C) and set the time for 5 minutes.
13. When cooking time is completed, remove the chicken wings and transfer them into a bowl.
14. Add the sauce and toss to coat well.
15. Serve immediately.

Tip:

If you are unable to find gochujang, then use Sriracha chili sauce.

Air fryer Chocolate Cake

Prep Time:	15 minutes	Calories:	351
Cook Time:	45 minutes	Fat (g):	16
Total Time:	1 hour	Protein (g):	6
Servings:	6	Carbs (g):	55

Ingredients:

- All-purpose flour — 1 cup
- Brown sugar — 6 oz (170g)
- Unsweetened cocoa powder — ½ cup
- Baking soda — ¾ teaspoons
- Baking powder — ¾ teaspoons
- Salt — ½ teaspoon
- Milk — ½ cup

- Vegetable oil   ¼ cup
- Large egg   1
- Vanilla extract   1 teaspoon
- Hot water   ½ cup

Instructions:

1. In a large bowl, mix the flour, sugar, cocoa powder, baking soda, baking powder, and salt and mix well.
2. Add the milk, oil, egg, and vanilla extract and gently stir the mixture until just combined.
3. Add the hot water and gently stir to combine.
4. Place the mixture into a baking pan and cover it with a piece of foil.
5. With a fork, poke holes on the foil.
6. Set the temperature of the air fryer to 350 degrees F (177 °C) to preheat.
7. After preheating, arrange the baking pan into the air fryer basket.
8. Slide the basket into the air fryer and immediately set the temperature of the air fryer to 320 degrees F (160 °C).
9. Set the time for 45 minutes.
10. After 35 minutes of cooking, remove the foil from the baking pan.
11. When cooking time is completed, remove the baking pan and place it onto a wire rack for about 10 minutes.
12. Carefully invert the cake onto the wire rack to cool completely before serving.
13. Cut into desired-sized slices and serve.

Tip:

Don't remove the cake from the pan before cooling for about 10 minutes; otherwise, the cake might fall apart.

Air fryer Chocolate Cupcakes

Prep Time:	15 minutes	Calories:	285
Cook Time:	20 minutes	Fat (g):	12
Total Time:	35 minutes	Protein (g):	3
Servings:	12	Carbs (g):	40

Ingredients:

For Cupcakes:

- Flour   1 cup
- Baking soda   ¾ teaspoon
- Baking powder   ¾ teaspoon
- Salt   ½ teaspoon
- Hot water   ½ cup
- Unsweetened cocoa powder   ½ cup

• Sugar	1 cup
• Milk	½ cup
• Vegetable oil	¼ cup
• Egg	1
• Vanilla extract	1 teaspoon

For Frosting:

• Butter, softened	8 tablespoons
• Powdered sugar	2 cups
• Cocoa powder	3 tablespoons
• Vanilla extract	¼ teaspoon
• Pinch of salt	
• Cream	3 tablespoons

Instructions:

1. Line 12 silicone cupcake holders with paper cupcake liners. Set aside.
2. In a bowl, mix the flour, baking soda, baking powder, and salt.
3. In another large bowl, add the hot water and cocoa powder and beat until well combined and smooth.
4. Add the sugar, milk, oil, egg, and vanilla extract and beat until well combined.
5. Add the flour mixture and mix until well combined.
6. Place the mixture into the prepared cupcake holders.
7. Set the temperature of the air fryer to 320 degrees F (160 °C) to preheat.
8. After preheating, arrange the cupcake holders into the air fryer basket.
9. Slide the basket into the air fryer and set the time for 12 minutes.
10. When cooking time is completed, remove the cupcake holders and place them onto a wire rack to cool completely before frosting.
11. Meanwhile, for frosting: in a bowl, add the butter, and with an electric mixer, beat on medium speed until soft and creamy.
12. Slowly add the powdered sugar and cocoa powder and beat until combined.
13. Add the vanilla extract and salt and beat until well combined.
14. Slowly add enough cream and beat until desired consistency is achieved.
15. Spread frosting over cooled cupcakes and serve.

Air fryer Chocolate Soufflé

Prep Time:	15 minutes	Calories:	417
Cook Time:	16 minutes	Fat (g):	31
Total Time:	31 minutes	Protein (g):	7
Servings:	2	Carbs (g):	35

Ingredients:

- Butter, melted   2 teaspoons
- Cocoa powder   1 tablespoon
- Chocolate, chopped   3 oz (85g)
- Butter, softened   ¼ cup
- Large eggs (yolks and whites separated)   2

- Sugar — 3 tablespoons
- Vanilla extract — ½ teaspoon
- All-purpose flour — 2 tablespoons

Instructions:

1. Brush the insides of 2 ramekins with melted butter and then dust each with cocoa powder evenly.
2. In a microwave-safe bowl, add the chocolate and butter and microwave on high for about 1½-2 minutes, stirring every 30 seconds.
3. Remove from the microwave and stir until smooth.
4. In another bowl, add the egg yolks and beat vigorously.
5. Add the sugar and vanilla extract and beat until well combined.
6. Add the chocolate mixture and mix until well combined.
7. Add the flour and mix until just combined.
8. In a clean glass bowl, beat the egg whites to the soft peak stage.
9. Add 1/3 of the whipped egg whites into the chocolate mixture and gently stir to combine.
10. Add remaining whipped egg whites in 2 portions and gently stir to combine.
11. Place the mixture into the prepared ramekins.
12. Set the temperature of the air fryer to 330 degrees F (165 °C) to preheat.
13. After preheating, arrange the ramekins into the air fryer basket.
14. Slide the basket into the air fryer and set the time for 14 minutes.
15. When cooking time is completed, remove the ramekins and serve immediately.

Tip:

Don't open the air fryer while cooking.

Air fryer Apple Crumble

Prep Time:	15 minutes	Calories:	197
Cook Time:	20 minutes	Fat (g):	6
Total Time:	35 minutes	Protein (g):	2.5
Servings:	4	Carbs (g):	35.6

Ingredients:

- Gala apples, cored and chopped   3 cups
- Almond flour, divided   3 tablespoons
- Pure maple syrup   1 tablespoon
- Fresh lemon juice   2 teaspoons
- Ground cinnamon   ½ teaspoon
- Quick oats   1/3 cup
- Brown sugar   ¼ cup
- Butter, melted   2 tablespoons

Instructions:

1. In a bowl, add the apple pieces, 1 tablespoon of the almond flour, maple syrup, lemon juice, cinnamon, and mix until well combined.
2. Place the apple mixture into the baking pan evenly.
3. In another bowl, add the remaining almond flour, oats, and brown sugar and mix well.
4. Add the melted butter and mix until a crumbly mixture forms.
5. Cover apple pieces with the oats mixture in the baking pan.
6. Set the temperature of the air fryer to 350 degrees F (177 °C) to preheat.
7. Arrange the baking pan into the air fryer basket.
8. After preheating, slide the basket into the air fryer and set the time for 20 minutes.
9. When cooking time is completed, remove the baking pan and set it aside to cool slightly before serving.

Tip:

Serve with vanilla ice cream or frozen yogurt.

Air fryer Baked Avocado Eggs

Prep Time:	10 minutes	Calories:	235
Cook Time:	9 minutes	Fat (g):	20
Total Time:	19 minutes	Protein (g):	8
Servings:	2	Carbs (g):	9.5

Ingredients:

- Avocado, peeled, halved, and pitted   1
- Eggs   2
- Salt and pepper   To taste
- Fresh parsley, chopped   1 teaspoon

Instructions:

1. With a spoon, scoop out some of the flesh from the avocado halves to make a hole.
2. Arrange the avocado halves onto a plate.
3. Crack 1 egg into each avocado half.
4. Switch on the air fryer, insert the fryer basket, grease it with olive oil, then set the cooking temperature to 400 degrees F (204 °C), and set frying time for 5 minutes or more to preheat the fryer.
5. After preheating, arrange the avocado halves into the air fry basket.
6. Slide the basket into the air fryer and set the time for 9 minutes.
7. When cooking time is completed, transfer the avocado halves onto serving plates.
8. Sprinkle with salt and black pepper.
9. Garnish with parsley and serve.

Air fryer Stuffed Mushrooms

Prep Time:	20 minutes	Calories:	313
Cook Time:	16 minutes	Fat (g):	26.7
Total Time:	36 minutes	Protein (g):	16
Servings:	8	Carbs (g):	3.8

Ingredients:

- Baby Portobello mushrooms   16 oz (453g)
- Cooked mild ground pork sausage   1 lb (453g)
- Cream cheese, softened   8 oz (227g)
- Parmesan cheese, grated   ¼ cup
- Fresh parsley, chopped   2 tablespoons
- Garlic clove, crushed   1

Instructions:

1. Remove the stems of mushrooms.
2. In a food processor, add the mushroom stems, sausage, cream cheese, Parmesan cheese, parsley, and garlic and pulse until chopped.
3. Stuff each mushroom with a sausage mixture.
4. Switch on the air fryer, insert the fryer basket, grease it with olive oil, then set the cooking temperature to 400 degrees F (204 °C), and set frying time for 5 minutes or more to preheat the fryer.
5. After preheating, arrange the mushrooms into the greased air fryer basket in 2 batches and spray with cooking spray.
6. Slide the basket into the air fryer and set the time for 8 minutes.
7. When cooking time is completed, remove the mushrooms and serve.

Tip:

You can use sausage of your choice.

Air fryer Pumpkin

Prep Time:	10 minutes	Calories:	52
Cook Time:	10 minutes	Fat (g):	0.5
Total Time:	20 minutes	Protein (g):	1.7
Servings:	4	Carbs (g):	12.3

Ingredients:

- Pumpkin, peeled and cut into ½-inch thick wedges   2 lbs (907g)
- Cooking spray
- Ground nutmeg   ½ teaspoon

Instructions:

1. Switch on the air fryer, insert the fryer basket, grease it with olive oil, then set the cooking temperature to 360 degrees F (182 °C) and set frying time for 5 minutes or more to preheat the fryer.
2. After preheating, arrange the pumpkin wedges into the air fryer basket and spray with the cooking spray.
3. Slide the basket into the air fryer and set the time for 10 minutes.
4. Shake the basket once halfway through.
5. When cooking time is completed, remove the pumpkin wedges and transfer them onto a platter.
6. Sprinkle with nutmeg and serve.

Air fryer Tuna Patties

Prep Time:	15 minutes	Calories:	103
Cook Time:	10 minutes	Fat (g):	3
Total Time:	25 minutes	Protein (g):	13
Servings:	10	Carbs (g):	5

Ingredients:

- Large eggs — 2
- Breadcrumbs — ½ cup
- Parmesan cheese, grated — 3 tablespoons
- Celery stalk, chopped finely — 1
- Onion, minced — 3 tablespoons
- Lemon zest, grated — 2 teaspoons
- Fresh lemon juice — 1 tablespoon

- Dried herbs   ½ teaspoon
- Garlic powder   ½ teaspoon
- Salt and pepper   To taste
- Canned albacore tuna, drained   15 oz (425g)
- Cooking spray

Instructions:

1. In a bowl, add all ingredients except for tuna and mix until well combined.
2. Add the tuna and gently stir to combine.
3. Make about 10 patties from the mixture.
4. Switch on the air fryer, insert the fryer basket, grease it with olive oil, then set the cooking temperature to 360 degrees F (182 °C) and set frying time for 5 minutes or more to preheat the fryer.
5. After preheating, arrange the patties into the greased air fryer basket and spray the top with cooking spray.
6. Slide the basket into the air fryer and set the time for 10 minutes.
7. Flip the patties once halfway through and spray the top with cooking spray.
8. When cooking time is completed, remove the patties and serve.

Air fryer Croutons

Prep Time:	10 minutes	Calories:	128
Cook Time:	7 minutes	Fat (g):	7
Total Time:	17 minutes	Protein (g):	3
Servings:	4	Carbs (g):	14

Ingredients:

- Butter, melted   2 tablespoons
- Dried parsley   1 teaspoon
- Seasoned salt   ½ teaspoon
- Garlic salt   ½ teaspoon
- Onion powder   ½ teaspoon
- Bread slices, cut into bite-sized pieces   4

Instructions:

1. In a bowl, add all ingredients except for bread pieces and mix well.
2. Add bread pieces and gently stir to combine.
3. Switch on the air fryer, insert the fryer basket, grease it with olive oil, then set the cooking temperature to 400 degrees F (204 °C), and set frying time for 5 minutes or more to preheat the fryer.
4. After preheating, arrange the bread pieces into the greased air fryer basket.
5. Slide the basket into the air fryer and set the time for 7 minutes.
6. When cooking time is completed, remove the bread pieces and serve.

Tip:

Feel free to use herbs of your choice.

Air fryer Lemon Brownies

Prep Time:	10 minutes	Calories:	391
Cook Time:	15 minutes	Fat (g):	18
Total Time:	25 minutes	Protein (g):	6
Servings:	4	Carbs (g):	56

Ingredients:

- All-purpose flour   ½ cup
- Sugar   ¾ cup
- Unsweetened cocoa powder   6 tablespoons
- Baking powder   ¼ teaspoon

- Salt   ¼ teaspoon
- Large eggs   2
- Unsalted butter, melted   ¼ cup
- Vegetable oil   1 tablespoon
- Vanilla extract   ½ teaspoon

Instructions:

1. In a large bowl, mix the flour, sugar, cocoa powder, baking powder, and salt.
2. Add the remaining ingredients and mix until well combined.
3. Place the mixture into a generously greased 7-inch baking pan.
4. Set the temperature of the air fryer to 330 degrees F (165 °C) to preheat.
5. After preheating, arrange the baking pan into the air fryer basket.
6. Slide the basket into the air fryer and set the time for 15 minutes.
7. When cooking time is completed, remove the baking pan and place it onto a wire rack to cool completely.
8. Cut into desired-sized squares and serve.

Air fryer Roasted Asian Broccoli

Prep Time:	15 minutes	Calories:	158
Cook Time:	20 minutes	Fat (g):	11
Total Time:	35 minutes	Protein (g):	6
Servings:	4	Carbs (g):	11

Ingredients:

- Broccoli, cut into florets   1 lb (453g)
- Garlic, minced   1 tablespoon
- Peanut oil   1½ tablespoons
- Salt   As required
- Soy sauce   2 tablespoons
- Sriracha   2 teaspoons
- Honey   2 teaspoons
- Rice vinegar   1 teaspoon

Instructions:

1. In a large bowl, add the broccoli florets, garlic, peanut oil, salt, and toss to coat well.
2. Switch on the air fryer, insert the fryer basket, grease it with olive oil, then set the cooking temperature to 400 degrees F (204 °C), and set frying time for 5 minutes or more to preheat the fryer.
3. After preheating, arrange the broccoli florets into the greased air fryer basket in a single layer.
4. Slide the basket into the air fryer and set the time for 15-20 minutes.
5. Toss the broccoli florets once halfway through.
6. Meanwhile, in a small, microwave-safe bowl, place the honey, soy sauce, Sriracha, and vinegar and mix well.
7. Microwave on high for about 10-15 seconds until the honey is melted.
8. Remove from the microwave and stir until smooth.
9. When cooking time is completed, remove the broccoli florets and transfer them into a large bowl.
10. Add the honey mixture and toss to coat well.
11. Serve immediately.

Tip:

For more taste, you can add a squeeze of lime juice.

Air fryer Jamaican Jerk Pork

Prep Time:	8 h 30 m	Calories:	238
Cook Time:	20 minutes	Fat (g):	9
Total Time:	8 h 50 m	Protein (g):	32
Servings:	4	Carbs (g):	0

Ingredients:

- Pork butt, cut into 3-inch pieces   1½ lbs (680g)
- Jerk paste   ¼ cup

Instructions:

1. Rub the pork pieces with jerk paste evenly.
2. Arrange the pork pieces into a baking pan and refrigerate to marinate for about 8-24 hours.
3. Remove the pork from the refrigerator and set it aside at room temperature for about 20 minutes before cooking.
4. Switch on the air fryer, insert the fryer basket, grease it with olive oil, then set the cooking temperature to 400 degrees F (204 °C), and set frying time for 5 minutes or more to preheat the fryer.
5. After preheating, arrange the pork pieces into the greased air fryer basket in a single layer.
6. Slide the basket into the air fryer and set the time for 20 minutes.
7. Flip the pork pieces once halfway through.
8. When cooking time is completed, remove the pork pieces and place them onto a cutting board for about 5-10 minutes before cutting.
9. Cut the pork pieces into desired-sized slices and serve.

Air fryer Blueberry Muffins

Prep Time:	10 minutes	Calories:	280
Cook Time:	14 minutes	Fat (g):	10.7
Total Time:	24 minutes	Protein (g):	4.4
Servings:	5	Carbs (g):	42.8

Ingredients:

- All-purpose flour   1 cup
- Sugar   ½ cup
- Baking powder   1 teaspoon
- Salt   ½ teaspoon
- Egg   1
- Butter, melted   ¼ cup
- Milk   ¼ cup
- Lemon juice   2 tablespoons

- Vanilla extract   1 teaspoon
- Fresh blueberries   ½ cup
- Lemon zest, grated   1 tablespoon

Instructions:

1. In a large bowl, place flour, sugar, baking powder, and salt and mix well.
2. Add the egg, butter, milk, lemon juice, and vanilla extract and mix until well combined.
3. Gently fold in the blueberries and lemon zest.
4. Place the mixture into the 5 silicone muffin holders.
5. Set the temperature of the air fryer to 330 degrees F (165 °C) to preheat.
6. After preheating, arrange the cupcake holders into the air fryer basket.
7. Slide the basket into the air fryer and set the time for 14 minutes.
8. When cooking time is completed, remove the cupcake holders and place them onto a wire rack to cool completely before serving.

Tip:

Feel free to use frozen blueberries.

Air fryer S'mores

Prep Time:	5 minutes	Calories:	251
Cook Time:	7 minutes	Fat (g):	13
Total Time:	12 minutes	Protein (g):	3
Servings:	2	Carbs (g):	30

Ingredients:

- Graham cracker, broken in half   2
- Marshmallow, broken in half   2
- Chocolate pieces   2

Instructions:

1. Arrange graham cracker halves into the prepared air fryer basket.
2. Place the marshmallow halves on the graham cracker halves.
3. Slide the basket into the air fryer and set the temperature of the air fryer to 390 degrees F (199 °C) for 5-7 minutes.
4. When cooking time is completed, remove the graham crackers and immediately arrange the chocolate pieces over the marshmallow.
5. Top with the remaining cracker halves and press lightly.
6. Serve immediately.

Printed in Great Britain
by Amazon

22147356R00117